CORVETTE
1953 to the present

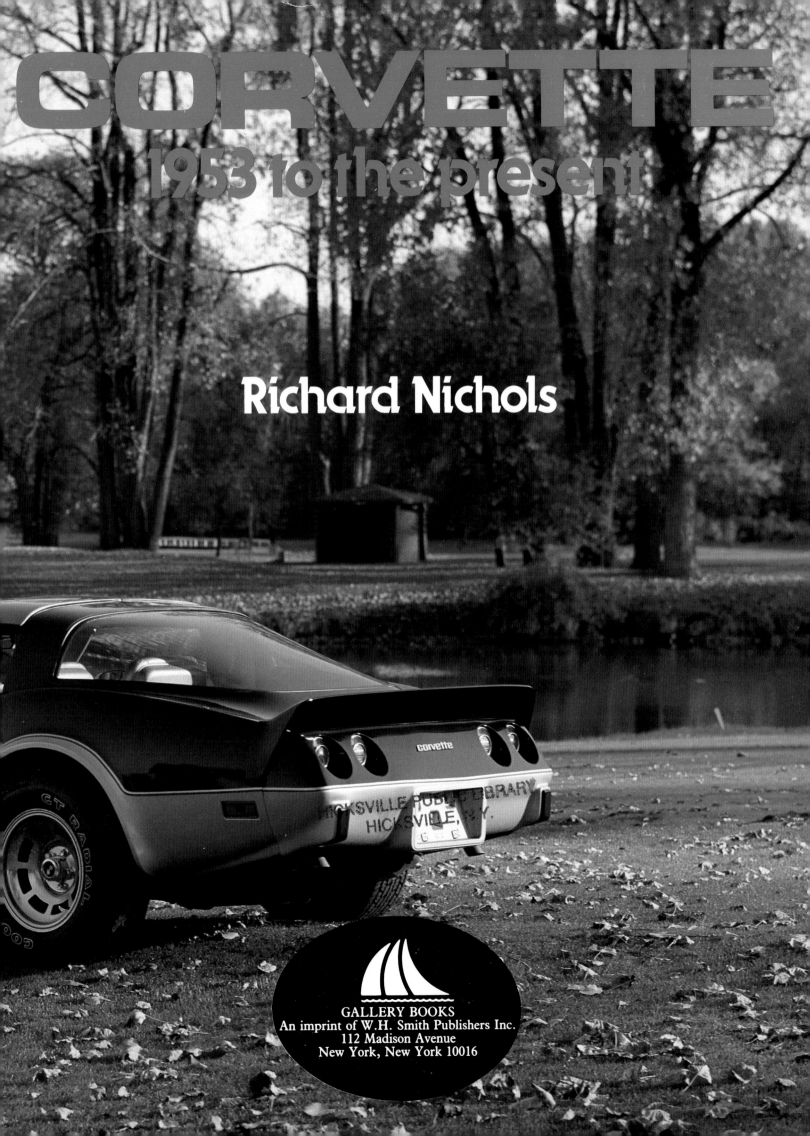

CORVETTE
1953 to the present

Richard Nichols

GALLERY BOOKS
An imprint of W.H. Smith Publishers Inc.
112 Madison Avenue
New York, New York 10016

Published by Gallery Books
A Division of W H Smith Publishers Inc.
112 Madison Avenue
New York, New York 10016

Produced by
Brompton Books Corp.
15 Sherwood Place
Greenwich, CT 06830

ISBN 0-8317-1788-2

Printed in Hong Kong

9 8 7 6 5 4

Contents

Introduction

The world is almost as full of writers of car books as it is of the books themselves, a circumstance that makes someone who is allowed to write about cars for a living extremely lucky indeed. Such persons are even luckier if they get the chance to write about cars they happen to like, as opposed to cars they happen to know a bit about – which makes me doubly lucky.

There can be few cars about which there are as many books as Corvette; the list, it seems, is virtually endless. This fact must be considered even more extraordinary when you recall that most auto books are about Porsche or Mercedes or Ferrari, or some other equally meritorious make of car with an interesting history. Corvette, on the other hand, is simply one product of the Chevrolet Division of General Motors; but this is not a book about Chevrolet which happens to include Corvette. It is a broad distinction and indicative of the glamor and esteem attached to this one marque.

Even more to the point is the situation at the GM Technical Center in Warren, Michigan. Researchers into Corvette history, while not exactly commonplace, are hardly an unknown quantity, and are accorded every facility and assistance by GM staff. There is a vast wealth of material available at the Tech Center, including photographs, and it dates right back to the beginning of the Corvette project. While I was there I expressed an interest in the Camaro, a car some ten years younger than the Corvette. But whereas the Corvette material occupies a number of filing cabinets, the file on Camaro can be picked up in one hand. This suggests that while everything that happened to Corvette from day one was scrupulously recorded, photographed and preserved, the same was not true of all GM products, even ten or twelve years later.

When I asked about this discrepancy, I was told that it was different; Camaro is only Camaro, but Corvette was – Corvette. The question is, back in 1953, when it was nothing more than a Dream Car on show at the New York Motorama, how did everybody who saw that Polo White convertible – from designers and builders and engineers to all the members of the public who lined up to look at it – how did any of them, never mind all of them, know then that they were looking at history being made?

Above: 1977 T-top contrasts with 1963 Sting Ray convertible *(below).*

The 1954 hardtop Dream Car.

Background

It is highly unusual to find any modern automobile to whose genesis one man can lay claim. Although committees, by reputation at least, design camels when horses are required, the skills needed to produce anything as complex and refined as the modern car are so diverse that one man cannot reasonably be expected to possess them all.

In the pioneering days of the industry, of course, the reverse was true, although most car makers found out fairly early on that even if the construction of vehicles was within their single capacity, the sales and marketing and the financial and administrative control probably were not.

It was exactly this kind of problem that beset the visionary dreams of William Crapo 'Billy' Durant. He built the vast General Motors conglomerate in his mind and set about creating the reality without heed to the pitfalls. His starting point was the ailing manufacturing company founded by Scotsman David Dunbar Buick in 1903. Durant lifted it from the mire and then brought it into his newly founded General Motors Company in September 1908. Six weeks later he included Oldsmobile, a year later Cadillac and Oakland (now Pontiac). Inside a year GM consisted of four manufacturing divisions plus the host of small component companies Durant had begun to absorb.

Under cash-flow pressure Durant was forced out of GM only two years after he founded it; his response was to form a partnership with race driver Louis Chevrolet. In March 1911 the first Chevrolet car, the Classic Six, appeared in a small shop on Grand River Avenue, Detroit. In their first full production year, 1912, Chevrolet built 2999 vehicles. In 1913 the company moved to larger premises in Flint, Michigan, ten miles from downtown Detroit; production went up to almost 6000 vehicles. Nearby were the Little Motor Car Company and The Mason Motor Car Company who at first made parts for Chevrolet; they were soon swallowed up by the acquisitive Durant. In 1914 the famous bow-tie trademark made its first appearance on the Royal Mail Roadster and in 1915, five years after start-up, the operation had expanded across the USA and Canada. Using Chevrolet stock, Durant bought his way back into GM.

Within the next few years Durant brought Chevrolet, Fisher Body and yet another myriad of component makers into the GM fold until cash shortage and the 1920 slump created a pressure to which Billy Durant once again was forced to bow, and he resigned from his company in November of that year. After several abortive attempts to launch new auto ventures of his own he died penniless, the manager of a bowling alley in Flint.

Under the firm hand of Pierre Du Pont the task of turning Durant's dream into reality was given to Alfred P. Sloan, and it was his sound business sense that gave GM the lasting base which they had needed for so long. But Sloan wasn't all dry columns of figures, and to him must go the bulk of the credit for one of the most significant car industry events of the twenties.

Harley Earl was born into the coachbuilding business. By the time he was old enough to take his place in the family firm, coachbuilding had given way to the Earl Automobile works in Los Angeles. This manufactured airplane fuselages and catered to the automotive tastes of the early denizens of the Hollywood orange groves. Harley Earl excelled at meeting their requirements; he designed streamlined

Top: The first Corvette Dream Car on its revolving stand at the Waldorf Astoria, 1953.
Above: Publicity shot of the same car. 'Corvette' hood script didn't make production *(below left).*

one-off bodies for their cars which were exhibited at the Los Angeles Auto Show – although having a clientele that included Fatty Arbuckle and Tom Mix did a lot to attract attention to his creations.

One of Earl's biggest clients was Cadillac dealer Don Lee. Through him he met Cadillac head man Lawrence Fisher, and it was Fisher who took Earl to Detroit; his arrival there coincided with GM's realization that the American demand for the automobile was growing larger and becoming more discerning. It was at this time that GM took the deliberate step of making sure that each year's model would be different from the last: the possibility that appearance could affect sales had just been noticed, and so they hired Harley Earl to design a car for them. The new La Salle which appeared in March 1927 was the first vehicle in Detroit to owe its appearance to a stylist.

In June of the same year Alfred P. Sloan founded a new department at GM: Art and Color. He invited Harley Earl to head it, a decision that would have far-reaching effects for Earl, the auto industry and the millions of Americans who would be driving his products – a number Sloan later estimated at an incredible 50 million.

GM entered the thirties with Chevrolet ranking second in the industry, behind Ford. Technical advances and concentrated styling improvements helped to change the situation as the decade progressed. Chevrolet passed the 10,000,000 units mark as they entered the 23rd year of production; 1934 was also the year that the 'Blue Flame' high-compression cylinder head was introduced. They made their way to top-seller in the industry in 1936, the year in which they completed construction of the world's largest body plant in Indianapolis.

In 1937 Harley Earl's Art and Color became the official GM styling department. Harley Earl was to be Vice-President in charge of Design with a huge staff reporting to him. However, he continued to exert his own personal influence over the appearance of all GM products, and his early involvement in and subsequent love-affair with flight was continually reflected in the sleek lines, curved glass and flamboyant wings which were the embodiment of auto styling in the fifties.

Almost all of it had been expressed before then, in the dream cars Earl designed: the Le Sabre, the Y-Job and the Buick XP-300 are probably the best-known. And it was through the medium of the dream cars and the Motorama showcase that Earl would get his next dream car off its revolving stand and out on to the street.

Motorama had been inaugurated in 1949 as a mobile display case which allowed potential customers a tantalizing look at the 'maybes' of the next decade, and a rather more realistic and cold-blooded look at the definite sheet metal for the following model year. The general idea, of course, was that some of the glitter and the glamor of the dream cars would rub off on the production hardware, with a consequent surge of orders. Indeed this was often the case, and although Motorama was essentially a showcase, cars were sold.

Television then was not the advertising medium it has since become, and this touring show was an extremely effective way of putting the product in front of the buyer. Traditionally the Motorama opened in the ballroom of the New York Waldorf-Astoria, stayed for ten days, and then went on a nationwide tour that took in Chicago, San Francisco, Los Angeles, Kansas City, Dallas and Miami.

Above: Early production at Flint. The completed body was dropped over the chassis and joined at 11 places.

It had been at the Los Angeles Motorama of 1951 that William Tritt's Glasspar Company had shown four designs all made from the new fiberglass material, which had benefited from a technology boom during World War II. It was followed by a *Life* article on the possibility of using GRP (Glass Reinforced Plastic, its correct appellation) for a vehicle body. All this coincided with the appearance of the dream car that would be the sensation of the 1953 Motorama.

As with so many other cars of character there are a number of simplistic tales that attempt to put the arrival of the new car down to a single cause, and establish a precise moment in time at which Harley Earl decided definitely that it would be designed, if not actually translated into metal.

Real life is seldom that simple, and things tend not to happen like that. Harley Earl was a vehicle designer, and possibilities for the future would have been a constant part of his life, as would the gradual,

almost subliminal acceptance of images that were going to influence him. It is unlikely that a picture of a jet fighter in a flying magazine was the spur that made him want to build a sportscar – although the shape may well have formed an impression on him. It is equally unlikely that a new awareness of the possibilities of fiberglass caused a sudden rush of blood to his brain, or that his first sight of the Alembic I show-car (follow-up to the original Glasspar Project) inspired him to rush off and design his own two-seater.

Other considerations aside, there were only six months between the appearance of Alembic I and Earl's sportscar, scarely more than

CORVETTE

the time elapsed since GM's official introduction to GRP following a demonstration by US Rubber.

What is certain, however, is that Harley Earl had excelled at swooping design since the twenties and was continually putting his expertise to work on projects that intrigued him. Equally certain was the flood of returning US servicemen who had come into close contact with the fleet-footed European sportscars during the war. With their appetites whetted they began to extol the virtues of this basic but exciting mode of transport.

In the main, the object of their attentions was the MG, and basic was a good word for it: rudimentary chassis, light but swoopy body, virtually no refinement, precious little weather equipment and an engine that amounted to little more than a tricked-up production unit with dual carbs.

All this was due for a change, and MG in particular launched a ferocious export drive in the immediate postwar years. After the 'export or die' exhortation of Lord Nuffield the company began to build cars with extra luxury specifically aimed at the newly-enthusiastic American market. This was followed by the arrival of Jaguar's new XK 120. Reputedly designed on a cigarette packet by a crowd of engineers sitting on a factory rooftop watching Birmingham being bombed during the war, the XK 120 was even more appealing than the MG had been. In fact it was so appealing that 90 percent of the sportscars were shipped straight across the Atlantic.

There is little doubt that the admiration which both MG and Jaguar attracted was a factor in Harley Earl's determination to design a two-seater. America hadn't had a sportscar of its own since the Mercer Raceabout, and had designed and built for a different market. Clearly Earl set out to prove that Detroit could be just as good as anybody else within the same design parameters, and throughout the project his design closely followed European practice.

Harley Earl had been working on this for some while before it became widely known and the dream car made its debut before the GM brass. Ed Cole was brought from Cadillac to be Chevrolet Chief Engineer in 1952; his reaction at first glimpse of the car in April of that year was later described as 'jumping up and down', and he promised Earl as much support as he needed to get the project pushed into production. Cole was one of the first Chevrolet people to see the car — although only a full-size plaster model had then been made.

Fortunately for Earl things were less than perfect in Detroit, or he might never have been able to push his design beyond that first closed showing. The effects of the Korean War had drastically reduced Chevrolet output downwards: from a high of two million in 1948 it fell to scarcely above one million in 1952. And although sporty imports accounted for a tiny fraction of the US market the attention they received was far out of proportion to their sales. In late 1952 an all-new, all-American two-seat sportscar was just what the GM doctor ordered to revive flagging sales.

Harley Earl, in cooperation with Charles Chayne, then head of GM Engineering, had already been responsible for the Le Sabre and the XP 300, both of which had been advanced two-seaters. The growing acceptance of the imported sportscar, especially among the young, led him to believe that such an item could become a production reality. He began toying with the project, involving several members of his design staff along the way. His idea was to produce a cheap two-seater which, despite being built in smaller numbers, would cost no more than an average sedan — less than $2000 at that time.

With a price constraint like that the car would clearly have to use as many stock parts as possible, and a stock frame, suspension and engine would need to be clothed in the right body. It would be a project with much visual appeal, but little of real sportscar character to recommend it to the enthusiasts. The project moved along in an unhurried manner for a while and then in early 1952 Earl caught his first glimpse of the fiberglass Alembic I. Fired with fresh enthusiasm, he put some extra energy into his own two-seater project, moving engineering design graduate Robert MacLean on to the job.

It was MacLean who threw the Detroit rule book out of his drafting-office window. Current practice dictated that a car was designed around its firewall. MacLean, however, scrapped that as an arbitrary

Harley Earl

The credit for Harley Earl's employment at General Motors as a stylist goes to the far sighted Alfred P. Sloan. It was he who warned his staff in the early twenties that as engineering advances slowed and stabilized, the appearance of an automobile could be critical to its success.

Harley Earl's family business was coachbuilding and it had grown to include custom-built car bodywork by the time the DuPont company had invented their first synthetic paint, called Duco. Sloan created another GM first, and made Harley Earl boss of a new 'Art and Color' section, the first styling house in Detroit.

Early connections with the movie industry led Earl into friendship with people like Cecil B. De Mille and Al Jolson, and these theatrical influences remained with him all his working life; Earl was the man who brought sculptor's modeling clay to Detroit from Hollywood. Up till then styling models had been made from wood, but clay gave the designers more freedom to work in complex curved shapes. Earl formulated the process of evolving a new car through the stages of drawing and then model making, which remains the norm today.

Known throughout the industry as 'Mister Earl', he also introduced to Detroit what was the biggest single influence on his own thinking, the fast-growing world of aviation. It was the twin-boom Lockheed P38 fighter that led Earl to introduce tailfins on GM cars, initially on a 1948 Cadillac. During the late fifties and early sixties the extent of Earl's influence had extended beyond GM to cover virtually everything built in Detroit. From the aviation world Earl introduced the wraparound windshield taken from the fighter's canopy, and brought the longer, lower, sleeker look to car styling generally.

Through the medium of the Motorama shows he created in the late forties Earl took his dream cars on the road across America. By this means he broke the public in to his way of thinking gradually, by showing them dream cars ahead of the production line changes that were coming in the next few model years. In the end this advance warning was unnecessary: Harley Earl was a man completely right for his time. Above all he gave his customers just one thing — imagery, which was precisely what the car buyers of the strong, confident and affluent postwar society wanted.

starting point, beginning his layout at the rear axle and then moving everything else in the car - passengers, firewall, engine and front axle – as far back and as low down as they would go. What he got was a 102in wheelbase, within which the engine sat 7in to the rear and 3in below its regular placement in the stock Chevrolet chassis.

This somewhat radical departure from the accepted norm was both good and bad. The most obvious factor was that it would make the new car a great deal more expensive than Earl had planned, simply because it could not longer use an existing Chevrolet frame: a special one would need to be designed and built, and as a low-volume unit it would be doubly expensive. On the positive side, the low center of gravity and almost even weight distribution (53 front/47 rear) that MacLean's layout allowed meant that the vehicle would have the potential to behave and handle like a genuine sportscar. Confronted with the layout, Harley Earl could have accepted or rejected it, for it was within his power to insist that the original plans, using an existing frame, should be adhered to. The more expensive purpose-built frame would almost certainly price the two-seater away from the college campuses at which it had been aimed, and would definitely reduce the number of potential customers for the production model.

Nevertheless, having satisfied himself that MacLean's layout was in keeping with the best traditions of European sportscar design, Harley Earl chose to stick with it. It was a decision that could either have made the car a short-lived financial success or - as it turned out – a lasting piece of automotive history. But it seemed likely that Earl was about to alienate his chosen youth market, and that his idea of saturating America with cheap two-seaters was not to be realized.

Above left: Chevrolet publicity shot taken on the Harbor Freeway in March of 1954, just prior to the Motorama opening.
Below: The ill-fated Corvair Dream Car.
Below right: The 1954 Dream Car with the hardtop which would reach production in '55.
Above right: The 1954 production Corvette.

CORVETTE

BACKGROUND

CORVETTE

There were still a number of ways in which the cost could be kept down, although none of them would be able to compensate for the big increase dictated by the cost of the new frame. At the time there were only a few styling sketches and ideas; none had yet crystallized or hardened and perhaps there were savings to be had along the way. Most of this work was done by Earl himself, and there is no doubt that the wraparound front screen was taken directly from his Le Sabre and had its roots in his love of aircraft.

But there was opportunity for the styling to match the engineering. MacLean's layout made the roofline low, 47in, which was in keeping again with European standards: most sportscars fell below 50in. The stylists kept the whole body low as well. Even thought the engine was set lower than usual within the frame, the hood was still so low that the front of the rocker cover had to be flattened to clear it. And the low-slung appearance was accentuated by the car's wide track, giving it a flattish look, which was yet another departure for an American design. In fact the 57-59in track was wider than Jaguar but narrower than Porsche, and thus adjudged acceptable.

A spare tire mounted on the outside rear deck was a feature of early design ideas, but this was gradually abandoned, falling by the wayside along with Harley Earl's plans to fit the headlights with clear Plexiglas covers which would blend in with the front fenders. The interior was given bucket seats and a central instrument cluster, in the European fashion. Then final details were ironed out before the clay was turned into a plaster model ready for display to top management for approval.

Present at that debut was Chevrolet General Manager Thomas Keating, Ed Cole (who had already seen the car), and GM President Harlow Curtice. The last-named was the driving force behind the Motorama shows and was keenly appreciative of their selling value. It is quite probable that he too had already had a sneak preview of the white-painted plaster convertible, but in any case he made an on-the-spot decision to build the car for the next Motorama and also to engineer a chassis to the point at which pre-production planning could begin.

In October 1953 the Detroit Section of the SAE met to hear a paper entitled 'The Evolution of a Sports Car.' It was read by the one key figure in the car's development who, up until its unveiling before Harlow Curtice in mid-1952, had not even seen it. In his paper,

Left: The full lineup for the 1954 Motorama.
Below: The original Dream Car, photographed before the Show had opened, even before its turntable had been completed.

Edward N. Cole

Ed Cole was a dedicated engineer and a tireless worker. Once he became involved in and committed to a project it received his continual undivided attention until it was completed. Even in his later days as a GM executive the shirt-sleeved Cole could often be found in a workshop until the small hours of the morning. His enthusiasm for whatever he was working on became almost legendary at GM and it made him a good salesman for his current projects. It was largely Cole who pushed the Corvair and the Wankel projects through the 14th floor at GM.

He started with GM in 1930, when he was 21 and rose through the ranks of the engineering staff to become a vice-president and Chevrolet general manager between 1956 and '61, and was president of GM from 1967 until his retirement in September of 1974.

During the time he was at Chevrolet the Corvette program received the immense benefits of his great engineering talent, enormous energy and boundless enthusiasm for Corvette itself. He'd come to Chevrolet from Cadillac, and had become excited by motor racing while preparing the Cunningham cars for the 1950 Le Mans 24 Hours. Chief engineer at Chevrolet from 1952 onward, it was Cole who pushed through, in a startlingly short time, the design and development of Chevrolet's first V8 engine for almost 40 years. The story of Cole's smallblock engine virtually demands a history book of its own. With 40 million-odd units built since 1955, it still remains the most popular V8 engine ever, probably the most popular engine of any kind.

During his time as Chevrolet boss it was Cole who promoted the dual-pronged road race development program for Corvette, encouraging the development of the fuel-injection system for the 283 smallblock, supporting the works race involvement and the Corvette SS, and turning a polite blind eye to the disdain with which the AMA edict was regarded by Corvette engineering staff.

After he moved on in 1961 Cole was replaced by the even more pro-racing Bunkie Knudsen, but by then he was busy finding more solutions to other engineering problems. It was under Cole, in fact, that the death knell of the musclecar era was heralded, following his decision to make a commitment to low-compression engines running 91-octane gasoline, which he knew would have to be the standard to cope with upcoming lead-free regulations.

After 44 years with GM Cole retired in late 1974 and died in an air crash in 1979, to the sorrow of all those who knew him and worked with him.

chassis engineer Maurice Olley said, 'On June 2 1952 Chevrolet engineers were shown a model of a proposed car of 102-inch wheelbase, for which a chassis was required. A complete car was to be exhibited at the Waldorf Show in January. There was not much time.'

Sketches for the frame were begun right away, and within ten days Olley had arrived at a design that needed only slight changes in order to meet the requirement; with minor alterations a sketch dated June 12 1952 was accepted as the final design. Using boxed sidemembers for strength, it had a solid crossmember (made possible by the high driveline) and weighed 213lbs. The body was mounted to it in 11 places and most of the components were taken directly from, or adapted from, Chevrolet parts.

The standard Chevrolet rear axle was mounted within the frame, and suspension was by four leaf springs, designed to allow a high (15 percent) roll understeer, which Olley felt was needed. Independent front suspension followed the standard Chevrolet pattern of parallel wishbones, coil-over-shocks and a sway bar.

Although rack-and-pinion steering was commonplace on the European sportscars, Chevrolet decided against it, providing instead their own 16:1 worm-drive linkage. In his address to the SAE in 1953, Olley explained that rack-and-pinion steering would have involved a ratio of 9 or 10 to 1. 'We regard this as too fast, even for a sportscar' he said.

The brakes were again stock Chevrolet items, although the master cylinder was given a bigger bore for better response to less pedal effort, and the balance ratio was altered to reflect the more or less 50/50 weight distribution the car was expected to demonstrate when loaded with two passengers and some luggage.

The knowledge that this was designed as a sportscar, and knowing the chassis was being designed to reflect this, and that an engine was being reworked for extra power, should perhaps have indicated that better brakes were needed. However, there wasn't time before the Motorama show nor, it later turned out, was there afterwards. The design team had virtually moved their drawing boards into the work-

shops and the chassis was being built from pencilled sketches almost the second they were finished. This was, as one engineer remarked, 'a crash program.'

Most of the European sportscars that Harley Earl and his team had looked at as they set about the details of the new car employed an existing production engine modified for a better power output. This was even true of Porsche, who used a design based around the Volkswagen air-cooled flat four. Even so, most units of this type developed around ¾hp per ci, whereas the average American engine, although bigger in capacity, was relatively less efficient, producing about ⅔hp per ci.

Not surprisingly, Chevrolet decided to follow the same ground plan, and the task of providing an efficient package for the car fell to Ed Cole, who performed near miracles with the faithful but ancient and plodding stovebolt six.

This had been a truck powerplant, and dated from 1941. In original stock trim, with a compression ratio of 7.5:1, it produced 115hp at 3600rpm from 235ci, which was less than ½hp per ci.. Maximum torque was 204ft/lbs, developed at 2400rpm, so that this engine could hardly be described as a screamer.

Cole raised the compression to 8:1 straight away, and then provided the engine with better breathing from an extremely high-lift cam, mechanical tappets and dual valve springs. The top-end strengthening was done because of the engine speeds which were 'known to exceed 5000 rpm' – high for the time. Three side-draft Carter carburetors were used, and a special dual-manifold exhaust design was used, which gave noticeable increases in mid-range torque.

For 1953 this engine was already destined to use a aluminum

All pictures: 1955 was the last year before Corvette's first facelift and, at 700 units, the lowest production year ever.

pistons, and altogether the changes made to it produced a respectable power increase, up now to about ⅔hp per ci: 150hp at 4200rpm with no noticeable increase in fuel consumption. Top speed was a theoretical 108mph.

Transmission for the car was the two-speed Powerglide, modified to handle the extra power. In order to accommodate the three carburetors under the hood the normal linkage had to be scrapped and the shift lever, instead of being on the steering column, was mounted on the tunnel. Defending the automatic transmission in late 1953, after it had been the subject of much criticism, Olley said that this had come from 'those who believe that sportscar enthusiasts want nothing but a four-speed crash shift. The answer is that the typical sportscar enthusiast, like the average man or the square root of minus one, is an imaginary quantity.'

It's still hard to define color availability exactly. '53 cars were all Polo White, there is some evidence for Sportsman Red in '54, changing to Gypsy Red in 1955, along with at least one metallic (Copper) and seven other colors.

Perhaps more significant was his prophetic observation that driving habits were already 'shifting away from the austerity of the pioneer toward the luxury of modern ideas'. Incredible as it may have been, the car was ready in time for its scheduled public airing, and a running model with a GRP body made from molds taken from the original full-size plaster model took the stage at the New York Motorama, scarcely six months after Harlow Curtice had approved that wood-and-plaster version.

The 1953 Motorama reputedly cost General Motors some $1,500,000 to stage. The centerpiece, revolving against a backdrop of the Manhattan skyline, was the white convertible dream car which had been named after a small, fast and highly maneuverable type of warship: Corvette.

The Press luncheon that marked the opening of the Show on January 16 was followed by its public opening, and it was claimed that more than 45,000 people attended on that first day alone. At the end of the six days GM said that 300,000 had passed through its doors and had placed $800,000 of orders for GM products. By the time the

CORVETTE

Motorama had completed its whistle-stop tour of the United States more than four million had seen the Corvette.

Visitors queued for hours just to catch a glimpse of the revolutionary new plastic sportscar and public interest in it was astoundingly high. Large numbers of inquiries about purchase were made at the shows themselves, and soon after that public debut letters of inquiry, many of them containing checks, began to arrive at Chevrolet's office in an increasing stream.

Market research confirmed that there was a serious potential market for the car, and it was largely this response that persuaded the company to go into production, although it was also clear that the lively and youthful image projected by the Corvette could do a great deal for their flagging sales and reputation. In April 1954 it was once again the redoubtable Maurice Olley who explained the Chevrolet reasoning in depth, this time via an address to the Marketing Association in New York.

He outlined quite clearly an important part of the GM rationale as he gave an appraisal of the market immediately prior to the arrival of Corvette. Jaguar, he said, had registered 3349 cars in the USA in 1952, 3914 in 1953. MG had sold 7449 and 6606 respectively, and even the brand-new Porsche had managed 141 and then 573. There was clearly a growing demand for two-seaters, which had been met by imports; 6000 in 1951, 11,500 in 1952 and 12,000 in 1953.

More importantly, these were by no means cheap cars. The Jaguar was priced at more than $4000, the M.G. at $2300 and the Porsche at $4600 at a time when the average American sedan was costing less than $2000. This was the original target price of the Corvette, and although its specially-built chassis dictated that it would have to be more expensive, it was clear that there was more than enough room for maneuver and ample room for some generous profit margins to be applied.

Quite aside from the financial element, there were other considerations, providing Chevrolet with fairly powerful motives for getting their own car into production. Not least among these was an element of national pride: 'How could the American automotive industry, with its tradition of achievement, allow European manufacturers to create and dominate a new market right in our own front yard?', Olley asked.

There was also the matter of publicity. The Motorama dream car had generated a huge welter of media coverage, and it was to be hoped that a production Corvette could continue to do the same thing for years to come. This was one of the reasons why Corvette development was to be on two levels: roadgoing production and racetrack experimental. It was precisely this kind of dual spearhead that had allowed the Europeans to get so far ahead in the first place, and Chevrolet would simply follow their well-established battle plan.

Thirdly there was the field of research. As Maurice Olley explained to the Marketing Association, Corvette had given Chevrolet a golden opportunity, a chance to 'explore thoroughly the field of reinforced plastics for automobile coachwork' on a low-volume production model. They were taking a bit of a chance with new technology, but not half the gamble it would have been had the plastic body been introduced on their 210 range with its 600,000-plus units. In other words they were using the Corvette as a mobile testbed.

It was an interesting philosophy and one that was to continue right up to the present day and would justify Corvette's continued existence when cold-blooded accountancy dictated its demise. Corvette's value as a proving ground would ensure its existence in years to come.

Some of what took place after the Waldorf show was dictated by necessity rather than by desire. Chevrolet had been toying with various manufacturing alternatives for vehicle bodywork and had almost decided on steel pressed by tooling made from a cheap metal alloy called Kirksite, although they still needed a long-term test. For a while it seemed likely that Corvette would be that test until it was found that the problems of tooling time-lapse and cost differed scarely at all from steel, and it was decided to produce the first batch of 300 Corvettes in the same GRP as the dream car. Even then the plan was only to use it for that first batch, and it was intended that fiberglass should be replaced by steel for 1954.

However, the persuasive and still embryonic fiberglass industry talked GM round in the end – the timescale of the Kirksite tooling was the deciding factor – and a first order was placed for 12,300 bodies, 300 immediately and 1000 a month due in 1954. The material had a rigid strength and was lighter than steel, did not rust, was capable of absorbing very minor bumps without deforming and was only 'somewhat' expensive at one dollar a pound, according to Maurice Olley.

Plans were laid to go into production with Corvette as quickly as possible: the object was to build at least 300 in 1953, delivery starting as early as possible. During the building of those first cars the production-line methods and techniques for dealing with the new material would be established. And the first cars would be made available in places where they could generate the maximum amount of follow-up publicity, rather than simply to the general public. They were earmarked for large dealer showrooms, race drivers and personalities with a high public visibility. Once they had been delivered manufacture would start in earnest in order to satisfy the vast demand that had now been created for America's first home-made sportscar.

1954. The wraparound bumpers completed the line of the chrome side trim, made Corvette look longer and lower.

The First Corvettes

There is a tendency to think of anything that has happened since the historical landmark of World War II – say since 1950 - as being comparatively modern. However, the relentless march of technological progress was artificially speeded up during the frenzy of the war years, and rather than slackening its pace has continued to accelerate. Today it is less a steady march, more a headlong gallop. The point is that, technologically speaking at least, 1953 was a very long time ago. So much has happened since then that is now taken for granted - but was, incredibly, unavailable 30 years ago.

The first commercial jetliner, the de Havilland Comet, flew in 1950. Nuclear power was used to generate electricity for the first time in 1951, at Arco, Idaho. In 1952 a Douglas airliner flew the Polar route over the North Atlantic for the first time; the first commercial jet service began to operate between Johannesburg and London; work began on the first atomic-powered submarine, USS *Nautilus*; the first hydrogen bomb was exploded; and the SS *United States* won the Blue Riband, crossing the Atlantic in three days, 10 hours. In 1953, Frank Sinatra started work on *From Here To Eternity* and the first experiments in color TV began and the Korean War drew to a close. It was a long time ago.

With no computers, no calculators, none of the sophisticated monitoring systems so common today, no instantaneous satellite communications (no satellites!), GM gave its engineers just five months - until June 1953 – to begin construction of an initial batch of 300 Corvettes in the revolutionary new GRP. It was a tall order.

Engineers looked at three ways of building the bodies, including the hand-laid method they had used for the dream car. Eventually they settled on a process of mating metal molds which offered speed, reliability and an acceptably long working life for the tooling. In April 1953, in Ashtabula, Ohio, Robert Morrison, who had perfected the method, formed The Molded Fiber Glass Body Company to meet the $4 million order for 12,300 bodies he had just received.

The plans for a steel body made with Kirksite dies had been abandoned, partly because of the timescale, partly because of its shorter working lifespan, partly because of the cost and partly because of the way the use of fiberglass in the dream car had fired the imaginations of those who saw it and wrote about it. Just tooling up in Kirksite would have cost more than the $4 million the whole order was worth to Morrison. The cost of the tooling in fiberglass - without the all-night work and subcontracted hand-laid molds needed to meet the June deadline – amounted to only one-tenth of that amount.

Even though Morrison anticipated no trouble in filling the 1000 per month order for 1954, still he had to bring in a subcontractor to help mold parts for that first 300, and still there was a great burning of midnight oil in Ohio.

The body consisted of 340lbs of fiberglass in 62 parts – 30 major panels and 32 smaller pieces – and as manufacture of these began it was necessary to find somewhere to mate them with the chassis and engine; at the time Corvette was little more than a homeless stray. The Chevrolet plant at St Louis was notified on March 28, 1953 that they would be expected to deal with long-term volume production of the new sportscar from the 1954 model year onward. Meanwhile a temporary home was needed.

Eventually a small area, just big enough to build the necessary three completed vehicles each day, was set aside in Flint. Here the body panels were glued together, painted, dropped over the chassis and fixed at 11 separate points.

It was crowded but it worked, and it served as a pilot to the main production line for which space was already being cleared in St Louis, where it would find a permanent home for the next 25 years. Meanwhile, the building of a Corvette was still a slow process.

All of those first 300 cars were identical: Polo White exterior, Sportsman Red interior, black top and whitewall tires. Apart from the fact that Chevrolet had already committed them to further promotion-

CORVETTE

Above: The rear licence plate was enclosed by a perspex cover which contained the radio antenna.
Below left: The recessed headlamps were protected by a chrome mesh screen.
Below right: The tail light was carried in a winged pod which was a complicated 3-piece molding.

al work in touring shows and dealer displays - making their similarity desirable if not vital – this uniformity provided the minimum distraction on the production line. Freed from the need to ensure correct trim with correct body color, plus adding any of the huge range of options available to the American car-buying public, the men on the line could concentrate on getting the build itself right and to a consistently acceptable quality. The whole body-making process was in its infancy, and fit and finish on the first 300 and more cars was far from being perfect. Just saying that the body panels were glued together before being dropped over the chassis is an expression that could conceal hours of patient filing and juggling.

The first few completed vehicles were regarded as pre-production prototypes and were handed over to Engineering for evaluation and testing. It was at this point that another of GRP's unusual – or unconsidered – qualities made itself known: plastic does not conduct electricity. In the automobile the two-wire system for a DC current is replaced by one wire: the entire body itself acts as ground/return. When Corvette's lights were switched on for the first time nothing happened. The return wires had been faithfully bolted to the plastic body, but the electrical system was completely inoperative, and a complete new wiring harness was required.

But with all its problems taken care of, and bang on schedule, Job One, as it was prosaically known, eventually rolled off the production line barely six months after the Motorama debut. In an industry that commonly takes three years or longer to gestate a new product, this represented an achievement which it would be hard to overestimate.

In Flint, Michigan, on June 30 1953, 12 months after its appearance as a plaster model, 12 months after Chevrolet engineers began to design a chassis for it, 12 months after engineers were asked to

produce an engine for it, and six months after it was shown to the public as a design exercise, Chevrolet body assembler Tony Kleiber drives the first sportscar manufactured by Chevrolet since the 1914 Royal Mail Roadster off the production line.

It has the same desirable qualities as the Motorama dream car — and many of its unfortunate drawbacks. Although it has the revolutionary new fiberglass body, and is extremely attractively styled, it has sidescreens rather than roll-up windows. It has a less than dramatic power unit in the stovebolt six, known as the Blue Flame six after the high-compression engines of the thirties, and it has two-speed automatic transmission. It costs $3400, putting it above the M.G. in price but below the Jaguar and Porsche. Yet it is not a sportscar in the accepted sense of the word.

Although most sports models imported into the USA feature an uprated engine in a near-stock chassis, with a dashing two-place body thrown on top, and although Corvette displays a similar treatment and makes a similar appeal, its performance is far from exhilarating. In fact many stock sedans can out-accelerate it with ease.

Yet Chevrolet plan to capitalize on the excitement generated by the Motorama shows, and to give it extra zest by sending one of the new cars to each of their national sales regions on a sales tour prior to releasing the remainder of the 300 models scheduled for 1953 production to VIP and 'personality' customers.

Some weeks after the first models ran off the line at Flint, but before the first eight were shipped out on their grand tour, Chevrolet invited a number of selected motoring writers to their Milford proving grounds, where each was given the chance to try the car over a seven-mile test course. This late September outing was Corvette's official Press launch, before a mere 50 journalists.

The day's event was hosted by Chevrolet General Manager Thomas Keating. Before the writers climbed into the vehicle Keating warned them that Corvette was 'not a racing car in the accepted sense that a European car is a race car. Rather we have built a sportscar in the American tradition, intended to satisfy the American public's conception of beauty, plus comfort, convenience and performance.' It was a theme that would be echoed over and over by various Chevrolet spokesmen as they saw their plans for market domination gradually crumble.

In fact it was Olley who, when addressing the Detroit SAE in late 1953, made most of the apologies necessary. Having said that one of the main points of interest about the new car was that it proved 'that it is possible for a great mass production organization to step out of its normal role of producing over 500 vehicles an hour to making 500 specialized vehicles in, say, two weeks', he continued 'This is an interesting fact even outside the United States, where it is generally considered that American manufacturing methods are too inflexible to meet modern conditions. This was well disproved within our own knowledge by the wartime performances of the automobile industry. It is proved to the world by such a specialized vehicle as the Corvette.'

Having said earlier in his paper that there was no need to apologize for the performance of Corvette (an opinion not altogether shared by everybody who drove it), Olley made the curious point that he did not want his paper to give the SAE the impression that 'the General Motors Corporation has lost all sense of decorum and is entering the racing car field' although that was to a large extent the impression they were relying on to sell the car.

But that part of the story was hardly going according to plan. Only about one in six of the people who had expressed interest in the

CORVETTE

1955. The V8 models *(above)* were distinguished from the sixes *(below left)* by the gold 'V' in their sidescript.

Corvette after seeing it at Motorama turned into what the industry would call firm prospects. It was clearly one thing to write and ask for information or tell a market researcher or a dealer that you would like to own a Corvette, an an altogether different matter when it came to parting with hard cash.

And not only was this attitude evident among the general public, but the VIPs for whom the almost 300 1953 models had been reserved also seemed less than desparate to own a Corvette. By the end of September l953 only 50 cars had been delivered to the VIP buyers, and total sales for the year made only 183 out of the projected 300. Chevrolet contented themselves with the knowledge that many of the cars were still going the rounds of dealer showrooms and were still being used for display purposes rather than being sold. And as September drew into Christmas and then the New Year it was still easy to think of a number of reasons why sales weren't up to target, easy to believe that they would soon pick up when spring was in the air.

Not until the summer of 1954 did Chevrolet properly face up to the fact that there was something drastically amiss. With 12,000 Corvettes scheduled that year they should have been making - and selling – 1000 every month. Only one half of the equation was working.

By this time production had moved out of Flint to St Louis, where the Corvette was being produced in ever-increasing numbers. After a slow, learning run of 15 cars in December of 1953, Edward Kelley, manufacturing manager for Chevrolet, announced that production had begun to rise. By May they were building 600 units per month and expected to make the full 1000 units a month in June – more than the total of all other American-built sportscars combined, more than all the sportscars imported the previous year, and apparently more than all the Chevrolet dealers combined could sell.

In the end the build rate was slowed to reflect the small demand for the model, and total production for the whole of 1954 amounted to only 3265 cars, about 2500 of which were actually sold. A deficit of that size could not fail to be missed, and it was clear that something somewhere was wrong.

THE FIRST CORVETTES

As 1954 wore on Chevrolet attempted a number of gambits aimed at putting the sparkle back into Corvette sales. From the time St Louis had taken over production the car had been available in a range of four solid colors, and there is some evidence that two metallics — green and bronze — were available as options.

It was on options that the next marketing ploy was worked. With its high price ($3400 FOB Flint) seen as a major sales hold-up Chevrolet dropped the ante closer to the M.G., giving it a $2774 recommended retail sticker. But although this was attractive at first sight, it became less so when the option boxes were taken into account. The two-speed Powerglide transmission was listed as a $178 option, but since no other transmission was available for Corvette it was clearly what might be called a mandatory option.

In midsummer 1954 Chevrolet dropped their restricted 'VIPs only' sales policy and were now trying hard to sell Corvettes to people 18 long months after the Motorama sensation and with very little follow-on publicity. In fact they did not even begin to place advertisements for Corvette in the automotive press until late in the year, and even then tried to maintain its exclusive 'for experts only' image. It was an uphill task, even though it had been helped as the first of the long-term tests conducted by the motoring press began to appear. In general the reception was warm. Though Corvette did not fall into the accepted mold of sportscar tradition it had other virtues and was acceptably fast. Top speed was over 100mph, and 0-60 times were in the 11-second bracket. It was, like the rest of the GM output, immensely reliable when compared to sensitive devices like Ferrari, and even Jaguar was held by a great body of opinion to be wanting in this department. However, America had not yet seen the widespread advent of the two-car family, and there were a limited number of people willing to choose a two-seater over a conventional sedan.

In strictly financial terms the Corvette was in deep trouble by the middle of 1954, and it was a widely held belief around GM headquarters that it would not last into the 1955 model year. However, there were a number of significant factors which, combined, managed to keep the accountants' ax at bay, delaying the apparently inevitable just long enough for Corvette to become its own salvation and gain complete control of its own destiny.

Of those significant factors one was a complete outsider, one was there right in the heart of GM, and the other was being hatched down the road at Dearborn, home of arch-rivals Ford. The latter had sat back and watched with interest as Chevrolet produced the Corvette out of a hat in New York — it had been given no pre-publicity, no build-up and no fanfares. They watched with even greater interest as Chevrolet then moved Corvette swiftly into production. Unwilling to

Good-looking to modern eyes, nevertheless initial sales success eluded Corvette until the advent of the V8.

CORVETTE

allow GM unrestricted access to a brand-new market occupied only by imports, Ford responded quickly and dramatically.

Ford plans for a two-seater had been laid before the appearance of Corvette. They too had seen the market and realized the demand for a domestic-built product that could rival the imports for performance plus romance, but was ultra-reliable and could in any case be repaired by the smallest local garage anywhere in America.

Ford market research, which had shown the existing gap by 1951, looked at the situation in far greater depth than Chevrolet, where the post-Motorama euphoria seems to have glossed over a number of cracks in the Corvette marketing plan. Announced in the fall of 1954 as a 1955 model, Ford's 'personal car' was the Thunderbird, and it came with a specification list and retail price that left Corvette a long way behind. Its power came from a 200hp V8 which drove through a choice of manual, overdrive or automatic transmission; straight away it had answered the two main criticisms of Corvette: lack of power and lack of a real transmission. More interestingly, the T-bird was a two-seat convertible (but with an optional hardtop) built on a 102in wheelbase, just like Corvette. Unlike Corvette, it arrived in the showrooms with a sticker price of less than $3000 and immediately began to sell in large numbers: more than 16,000 in its first full year, 1955. The previous year Corvette had sold 2500 and entered 1955 with a surplus of 1000 vehicles. During 1955 only 674 Corvettes would be built and not all of the 1600-plus total inventory would be sold.

Having entered a new market, Chevrolet were about to find themselves being thoroughly whipped by a rival who came into it a whole year behind them and promptly outsold them ten to one. If there had been doubts around GM headquarters about the viability of the market they had just entered then Ford's success in it quashed them right away. Clearly market research had been correct, and clearly there was a market there. Equally clear, therefore, was the logical deduction that if the research was right, Corvette was wrong.

Maurice Olley had expressed GM policy once before when he had said that they would not allow foreigners to create and dominate a new market on their doorstep. Nor would they allow Ford that privilege now. Rather than drop Corvette and back off, investment in it would be increased and the Ford challange answered.

With the decision to retain Corvette taken, the next step was to make it the car it should have been in the first place, by giving it an engine capable of the right level of performance.

Chevrolet hadn't made a V8 engine for years. In fact they hadn't made a performance engine of any kind for years, and Ford's flathead more or less ruled the performance roost, as it had done since 1932. But those who gave Ford all the credit for leading the way were slightly off-center. Credit for that rightfully belongs to the 55hp ohv 288ci V8 engine, which for a production run slightly longer than a year powered the Chevrolet Model D of 1917.

Thirty-eight years later Chevrolet re-entered the V8 performance world with a design that would become the most successful V8 engine ever; in fact it is the most successful engine of any kind ever, with total production close to 40 million units. One of the most effective and efficient V8s, it was also easy to produce, possessed of huge tuning potential and arrived just in time to provide the Corvette with the performance it needed to survive.

It is untrue to say that the engine was developed especially for Corvette. In fact, it was under development before Corvette was off the drafting board and before Ed Cole arrived at Chevrolet, although he was responsible for a great deal of work on the engine. However, it clearly was exactly right for the Corvette and an early version of this V8 was fitted to the Motorama dream car late in 1953. The effect was as satisfactory was everybody expected, but it wasn't until the 1955 model year that the engine was available and Corvette acquired it along with the rest of the division's vehicles.

Chevrolet were virtually alone in not having a performance engine, alone in not having a V8. At the time the V8 was the touchstone of the performance world; brute power, particularly in terms of straight-line acceleration, has always ranked high among automotive criteria – and with gasoline then about 30 cents a gallon.

Zora Arkus Duntov

More than any other person Zora Arkus Duntov is the man associated most closely with the Corvette in the minds of onlookers. Above all others, Duntov is the man we know as 'Mr Corvette'. Considering the fact that its creation was nothing to do with him, this unofficial title is a clear indication of the influence he exerted over it during his twenty years' involvement with the program.

In many ways a separate biography of Duntov is fairly superfluous within any history of the car, since his life and Corvette's are inextricably woven for a good two-thirds of the tale. Indeed, it would be hard to imagine there being any story to tell were it not for the engineering brilliance and single-minded dedication of this Russian emigre. Though the original inspiration was Earl's, the power Cole's and the dashing appearance of the sixties Mitchell's, it was Duntov who pushed Corvette engineering to its limits, and it was only the vast corporate nature of the GM structure that prevented him from realizing his ambitions for Corvette in pure engineering terms.

It is in fact safe to say that the long-awaited Corvette restyle, which finally emerged in the 1984 models, would have come a great deal earlier and would have been in the form of a mid-engined radical had it not been for the retirement of Duntov, Cole and Mitchell in 1975. Duntov himself ascribed a large part of the premature demise of the beautiful mid-engined Aerovette to Ed Cole's championship of the Wankel rotary engine, dropped by GM after it became clear that the early models simply weren't going to make it through the increasingly stringent emission-control regulations.

After his retirement from GM – 'they must have been happy to get rid of me', he told *Autoweek* in 1978 – the maverick Duntov, whose unorthodox behind-the-wheel activities at places like Pike's Peak and Daytona and continual disregard of the AMA ban, had often rankled on the 14th floor and left him noticeably out of place in the pin-striped uniformity of the General Motors hierarchy, went on to work on a number of different projects. Mostly it was pure engineering research, but he followed his belief in the value of the mid-engined layout faithfully, putting in a considerable amount of time in wind-tunnel testing a new sportscar then on the drafting boards of a company formed by yet another ex-GM rebel, the colorful John DeLorean.

Still 'retired', Duntov continues research into gas-efficient engines from his home in Detroit.

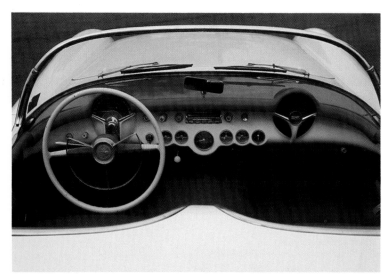

Top left: Although it looks pleasing, the dash layout was often criticized.
Left: Probably the longest surviving wheel disk in automobile history.
Above: Corvette had to wait for 12-volt lighting and electrics.
Below: A 1955 Corvette with soft top and whitewall tires.

CORVETTE

Work on Chevrolet's V8 engine was begun by Ed Cole's predecessor, E. H. Kelley, and Cole simply carried on with it: in that respect he is not the originator of the project, although his personal input has earned him widespread acclaim as the 'father' of the smallblock engine. As laid down by Kelley the V8 would have been a lower-capacity unit than the six it was to replace, and it was Cole who straight away changed that, enlarging it from 231 to 265ci. In an effort to achieve light weight with small overall dimensions and low cost the engine was designed with cylinder walls and water jackets much thinner than anything else seen in Detroit, even within GM, at the time – although it has since become accepted practice in the industry. The intake manifold also doubled as the cover for the lifter valley, a job previously handled by a separate casting, and the valve gear itself was a lightweight stamping. The cylinder block featured a low deck height and the small crankshaft had the shortest stroke around.

Chevrolet were rightly very pleased with themselves by the time the engine was finished, although it is entirely possible that even they were then unaware of the full extent of the achievement. Many of the features they had included in the design to save cost were precisely those that gave the V8 its vast powerhouse potential.

Stripped of accessories the engine weighed in at about 40lbs less than the antiquated stovebolt six it was replacing, which represented a positive advantage all round. The short stroke meant shorter (and lighter) conrods; with its lightweight valve train it could rev higher than any other V8 in Detroit, going to over 6000rpm while the others were lucky to exceed 5000 without hurting. The combination manifold/valley cover sat high over the intake ports, allowing better breathing than before, and the wedge-shaped heads worked well in stock trim, and responded even better to raised compression.

In stock form this was the engine that Chevrolet made available across their range, including the classic sedans which came from the same GM design studios that were responsible for Corvette's appearance. In the bigger passenger cars the V8 had a l60hp base unit and a more powerful, 180hp option, but in Corvette (now externally distinguished by the addition of a 'V' to the crossed-flags badge and a side script which read CorVette instead of Corvette) there was the high-performance version with dual exhausts and Carter 4-bbl

carburetor. This combination produced maximum torque of 260lbs/ft at a satisfactory 3000rpm and lifted Corvette up to 195hp at 5000rpm, giving it a top speed of about 118mph. Better, it ran 16-second quarters and did 0-60 in 8.8 seconds, clipping a good 3 seconds off the best the straight six could manage, and almost the same amount off the best times anybody could produce for Ford's new Thunderbird.

The substantial facelifts Harley Earl had been planning for the '55 models didn't materialize: quite apart from the poor record of Corvette, Chevrolet had spent heavily on tooling for the new 1955 sedans, making differences between the 1954 and '55 versions few. Although the V8 had transformed Corvette completely it still looked the same. Virtually all of the 700 models built during 1955 were given the V8 engine (the six was still available), but news of the changes to its nature took time to travel.

Among the people who saw the Corvette revolving on its Motorama turntable was a 43-year-old engineer who was at the time involved with Sidney Allard's race team, but was better known in America for his hemi-head conversion of the flathead Ford V8. The Ardun heads were named after him. Zora Arkus Duntov was a Russian, born in Belgium where his father was an engineering student.

He grew up in what was then Petrograd and there attended the Petrograd Electro-Technical Institute. He returned to Western Europe after the Revolution and obtained a degree in Mechanical Engineering, remaining in Germany to work in his chosen profession. He made his first professional contacts with the internal combustion engine working on diesels and supercharger units, and gradually became involved with race cars, first at the design level and then from the more practical point of view - behind the wheel. His theories on supercharging were way ahead of their time, and his gift for performance engines was recognized straight away.

He joined the French Air Force when World War II broke out, and made his way to America when France surrendered. It was after the war that he doubled the ouput of the 20-year-old flathead Ford V8 engine with an ohc hemi-head conversion. Duntov spotted the strength of the Ford's bottom end, and realized that it was capable of

THE FIRST CORVETTES

revving a great deal faster than stock if it was given the opportunity. His aluminum heads lifted the output far above the stock engine's lowly 85hp and his belief in its great strength was more than justified; blown flatheads with the Ardun conversion have produced 500hp.

Having seen and admired the Corvette at the Waldorf Astoria in January 1953, Duntov began a correspondence with Ed Cole which led to his employment as a member of the Chevrolet Research and Development staff in the spring of the same year. While he was there he began to 'tinker' with a Corvette prototype in the workshop; giving it a workout at the Milford proving grounds he found that its handling left a great deal to be desired. His modifications to the back of the prototype were simple enough, based around the high rear-end roll oversteer combined with front understeer. Duntov corrected the situation by limiting rear spring travel and adding a stabilizer to the front end: simple enough changes, but they had exactly the desired effect, tidying up the handling no end.

His unofficial twiddling with Corvette became more and more frequent and more and more official. Maurice Olley asked him to look at the problem that was affecting the back end of the car, where exhaust gases were staining the fenders. Duntov conducted some early (and primitive) but effective aerodynamic tests with tufts of wool, discovered the source of the problem and solved it by moving the exhaust outlets to the tips of the fenders.

His unofficial status became more and more official over the years, until he was given responsiblity for Corvette engine and chassis in 1963, confirming a situation that already existed, and was named Chief Engineer of Corvette in 1968. Over the 20 years or so that he was associated with Corvette Duntov grew into a legendary figure, became known as 'Mr Corvette', and a selection of puns perpetrated in a variety of automobile magazines confirmed his status as the headlines gradually changed and 'The Mark of Zora' became 'The Marque of Zora'.

The first of his many personal touches on the car were the handling

CORVETTE

Above: The dual exhausts exited from the rear bodywork.
Left: 'Aerodynamic' fins on the rear light pods were less effective than appealing.
Far left: The 1956 dual-quad small block V8.

details which he had corrected out of curiosity at Milford, and the relocated exhausts. Together with his answer to one other important criticism of the Corvette - the lack of proper roll-up windows and the addition of real door handles on the outside – these should have appeared in the 1955 facelift, for which Harley Earl had prepared a new grille and angled fender vents behind the front wheels. But there was no facelift for 1955.

Although the revamped Corvette had to wait another year, while the rest of the Chevrolet passenger cars went into the first of what are now regarded as the three classic seasons of 1955-57, the new V8 was offered on Corvette as an option instead of the Blue Flame six, at an additional $110. Production figures for the year were well down on 1954, at 1639, but even so the buying public voted the stovebolt six straight out of the back door: less than ten people chose it in preference to the new V8 powerplant.

By 1956 the tooling costs of the new passenger car lines had been absorbed for all practical purposes. That meant Chevrolet could spare time, effort and money to look a little more closely at their hybrid little sportscar, which seemed to be on the verge of slipping from sight altogether. Ford, however, were doing well with the Thunderbird, and as Corvette sales dropped back the T-bird marched onwards, outselling Corvette by ten to one in 1955. Almost as soon as that became clear during the course of the year, Harley Earl showed his designs for a restyled Corvette to the GM management and got almost instant approval to go into production for the following year.

This excellent decision not only proved to be the salvation of Corvette as a whole, but it released one of the most elegant of automobiles on to the roads. Years later these Corvettes are still properly regarded as classic of the breed.

THE FIRST CORVETTES

The long-awaited facelift makes Corvette sleeker, leaner than before.

The Real McCoy

Almost certainly it was Ford's success with the Thunderbird that pushed Corvette into its third year. With the tooling for the passenger cars successfully completed the year before, and with the V8 engine costs also built into 1955, there was now room for Chevrolet to put some investment into Corvette, and it was thus in the '56 model year that it finally came of age. There is a widely-held belief that restyles of Corvette only become settled in the second year of production when the factory gets into the groove and all the minor bugs have been ironed out: the first year's production of a new model has traditionally been troublesome.

True or not, the '56 is the Corvette that many enthusiasts and collectors choose as being the most desirable. Probably that's because it was the earliest model in which everything came together right. Coincidentally, it was the first to bear the personal hallmark of Zora Arkus Duntov, an imprint that was to be a recognized sign of excellence for the next 20 years.

The basic shape of the new body had been established in early 1955. Although its appearance still clearly identified it as a member of the Corvette 'family', there was virtually no feature of the original car carried over to the new apart from the grille. That said, the head-on appearance of the two cars was remarkably similar, although this was the only view that remained so.

The recessed headlights were brought forward to the leading edge of a more conventionally-shaped fender, while the rear lights, mounted on an embryonic 'fin', were cleaned up and recessed into the downward curve of the rear fender. The result was a leaner, sharper profile, given an even harder edge by the optional hardtop. The exhaust outlets were moved to the edge of the fender where they were incorporated into the bumper guards. Early styling possibilities here had allowed them an exit through the side of the fender just behind the rear wheel.

For the first time Corvette had a door handle on the outside. Traditionally, sportscars with side curtains rather than proper roll-up windows had no need of an external handle since it was just as easy to unbutton the curtain and reach inside, but for 1956 all that had to change. Incorporated into the 1956 Corvette were Duntov's roll-up windows (with a power option); a pair of small air intakes which had sat on the front fenders just ahead of the windshield on the Motorama

car, but had not appeared on production cars until now; and gentle but visible hood bulges. The wheel disks were designed to look like knock-on wheels and were so popular that they remained on the car until 1962, an almost unheard-of run for a normally transitory item.

Also introduced in 1956 and given a long production run were the side scallops. Like the original wraparound screen, these were very much a hangover from the La Salle dream car, although the screen appeared on the original and the scallops on La Salle 11 which made its debut at the '55 Motorama, scarely a month before the Corvette revamp was finalized. These were to become one of the most long-lived styling features of Corvette, alongside its dual headlights (introduced in 1958) and dual round rear lights (introduced in '61). The scallops have survived in production right up to the present day, although in a rather low-key form. In fact they have grown progressively smaller over the years until today only a suggestion of them remains in the small slots behind the front wheel.

In 1956, however, they were large, bold indentations, designed to

Above: Duntov at the wheel of the V8-engined '54 car during testing at GM proving grounds.
Right: Duntov accelerates away from the flag at Daytona.
Below: Daytona, February 1956. Betty Skelton, Duntov, John Fitch.

CORVETTE

echo the full-fendered sweep of the classic sportsters of the thirties; painted in a contrasting color to the rest of the body, they did just that. The flexibility allowed by working in fiberglass meant that final approval of the 1956 body shape could be delayed until quite late in the year. Although basic agreement had been reached in February the chrome trim edging the side scallops was added much later on.

Significant alterations were also made underneath Corvette's brand-new skin. The minor changes that Duntov had made to the suspension geometry after his test drives at Milford were included on the production line, making the 1956 model the first Corvette capable of demonstrating the handling qualities of a true sportscar.

It must be said that this kind of handling could never have been achieved in the original Corvette in any case. The arrival of the V8 made a world of difference since it weighed 40lbs less than the Blue Flame Six and enabled a substantial change to be made to the weight distribution. The 1956 Corvette now balanced out 52 front/48 rear.

In addition the performance of the V8 was stepped up over the previous year. In stock trim it gave 210hp at 5200rpm, the bulk of the extra power coming from a revised cylinder head which gave it an increased compression ratio, up from 8:1 to 9.25:1. There were more improvements all round, including new, larger-bore exhaust manifolds, better exhaust valves and a new dual-point distributor to deal with higher rpm without crossfire.

On top of the stock engine there was also the option of dual Carter 4-bbl carburetors instead of one. This version really put the Corvette into the high-performance bracket, with a power output of 225hp at 5200rpm, and maximum torque up to 270ft/lbs at 3600rpm.

With this power installed under its hood the Corvette did 0-60 in

THE REAL McCOY

CORVETTE

The 1956 cars *(top left and main picture)* changed little into '57 *(top center)*, although the crossed flags and side script give away the presence of fuel injection.
Top right: By 1959 there were dual headlamps and a revised dash. The T-handle on the shift lever was introduced this year to prevent unintentional reverse shifting.

THE REAL McCOY

CORVETTE

only 7.4 seconds, managed 15.9/88mph quarters and had a rewarding top speed of 129mph. It was much aided in reaching these figures by – at last – the arrival of a three-speed manual gearbox and a large-diameter clutch made lighter in use by the fitting of multiple coil springs rather than a single diaphragm spring.

The improved performance the new combination allowed produced the sort of figures that Corvette needed to establish its credentials as a sportscar – but they had to be made public, and in the right way. Unlike its European competitors - and Mercedes was now added to a list that already included M.G., Jaguar and Porsche – Corvette had no track record with which to prove its performance and establish its identity in the public mind. Fortunately it did have, in the shape of Zora Arkus Duntov, the right person to create that history.

Despite the working flexibility of fiberglass the 1956 Corvette was something of a late developer, making its debut at the Waldorf Astoria for the Motorama show in January 1956: traditionally the season's new models make their first appearance in the fall of the preceding year.

Still, there it was on the turntable, looking every inch the part, low and sleek, with the faint beginnings of that kick-up over the rear fender that would later become one of Corvette's visual trademarks.

It carried a sticker price only marginally over $3000 without options. All it needed was...proof.

In 1955 Ed Cole and Duntov had discovered a joint interest in promoting the good news about the forthcoming Corvette revisions through racing or speed trials. Late in 1955 Duntov took a heavily-disguised 1956 Corvette to Pike's Peak, making a record climb of 17 minutes 24 seconds. Cole and Duntov agreed that a public performance of this nature was precisely what was needed to establish Corvette properly for the ranks of the enthusiast buyers who tended to notice competition results.

The plan was to develop Corvette along similar lines to Jaguar, running a racing-development program to garner publicity and improve the breed alongside, but separate from, the production line cars. Pike's Peak had been the first physical evidence of that program and now, in early 1956, Duntov would produce the second; this time it would be no secret.

Duntov chose a straightforward high-speed run for his attention-

Main picture: Corvette #4, driven by Dick Thompson and Gaston Andrey, winners of the GT class at Sebring, 1957.
Inset: Cumberland, Maryland, in 1960.

THE REAL McCOY

grabber, with Daytona as the venue, and began tests with a 1954 V8 prototype. He felt that he needed to run at 150mph to establish Corvette's bona fides and that therefore he required more horsepower than even the 1956 Power Pack V8 was delivering. His solution was to design a new camshaft to release this power from the engine, and while he waited for official approval he ran tests to see how much drag he could remove from the car by taping the grille and using a small screen instead of the full windshield.

He had to wait for approval of the new cam because of its unorthodox nature. Although it gave a higher lift than the stock item, it was lower than the Power Pack by a noticeable amount. But its broad lobes gave it a tremendous duration, allowing the engine the opportunity to indulge in some ferociously heavy breathing. The stock cam inlet opened 12 degrees before TDC and closed 54 degrees after BDC. The Power Pack cam increased that enormously, to 22 and 63 degrees respectively. Duntov stretched it even further, to a massive 35 and 72 degrees, making similarly-proportioned increases to the exhaust valve timing.

When he finally got a prototype delivered and fitted, it produced precisely the desired effect, boosting the V8 up to 6500rpm with no valve bounce and allowing a theoretical maximum top speed of 163mph at 6300 rpm from its 240hp. Suitably armed, Duntov and his team set off for Daytona Beach late in 1955.

The weather was against them from the moment they arrived, and the hoped-for record was not forthcoming. The year 1955 eased into 1956, and the new car made its debut at the Waldorf. And it was then, as the show car revolved on its turntable, that the news arrived from

Daytona: despite adverse conditions Duntov had run a two-way record-breaking average of 150.583mph on a loose-packed sand surface that gave him little help.

It was the medicine exactly as prescribed, and with one success under the belt Chevrolet set out to repeat the dosage, arriving at the official NASCAR Speed Week in February with three cars. Two were handled by racers Betty Skelton and John Fitch, and a third car was allocated to Duntov. This was the January record-breaker, now sporting a 10.3:1 head reckoned to provide about 255hp, and entered in the Modified category.

For the first time Chevrolet and Ford factory teams came face to face; the Thunderbirds were also at Daytona. Motor Trend reported that eagerness to establish new records led to a more than passing amount of rule-bending. NASCAR officials were kept on their toes for the whole time, but they stayed on top of the task and the eventual winners and record holders were more or less legitimate.

At the end of the week the honors were mixed. Thunderbirds took the first two places in the standing-mile acceleration tests; at 88.779mph the winner Chuck Daigh was almost 2mph faster than Fitch's third-placed Corvette at 86.872mph. Duntov's Corvette was the fastest Modified and fastest overall - at 89.753mph - for the standing mile, and in the flying mile Fitch ran fastest at 145.543mph, with Betty Skelton next at 137.773mph. Duntov was the quickest Modified again at 147.3mph, strong wind preventing him from matching his previous record. The Modified car did l56mph on its downwind run, a top speed bettered only by a Grand Prix Ferrari, and that by less than lmph.

The figures were good enough to mark the arrival of Corvette as 'America's only genuine production sportscar' – that was Chevrolet's advertising claim. It was also good enough to attract the attention of Washington dentist Dr Richard Thompson. In the spring of 1956 he forsook his regular Jaguar mount and began campaigning a Corvette

Below: The Sebring hangars in 1957, as the SR2 gets attention to the troublesome rearend. Brake drums are visible in the wheel wells.

Above: Close work in B Production.

in the SCCA C Production class. Although Chevrolet's racing involvement through Corvette was official, it was always low key, even in the days before the AMA interdict, and often took the form of behind-the-scenes help to privateer entrants rather than full-scale works team entries. With the help of Chevrolet in general and Duntov in particular, Thompson secured the 1956 Group C championship for Corvette.

But even before that, the Chevrolet company established yet another landmark for Corvette. With straight speed trials behind them Duntov and the Corvette team headed for fresh race involvement at Sebring in March 1956.

By comparison to the roughhouse of circuit racing the speed trials had been easy enough. As a general rule for speed trials, what tests out on the bench and the proving ground will work out on the day. But racetracks are their own testbeds and proving grounds, and it is here that what has been tried back at the factory must be fully tested for the first time, with no guarantee of success.

At that time the prestigious international road races were held in Europe: the Mille Miglia, the Targa Florio, the Le Mans 24 Hours. Then the disused airport at Sebring, Florida, was turned over to racing and almost immediately the 12-hour event established itself as one of the most glamorous races in America.

The team who had been to Daytona in January had tried out a Corvette at Sebring while they were in the area, and in February the decision to enter the March 12 Hours was taken. A four-car squad was entered by a private team from Illinois with full-scale factory involvement hiding behind this thin veil of secrecy.

Three of the cars were 265 Power Pack versions running the Duntov cam; the fourth was bored to 307 inches to lift it into Group B. All shared two common problems: an almost total lack of high-speed braking and a carburetor imbalance which meant that they could be set up to run properly in heat or cool, but not both. The latter fault was already well-known in Detroit and no solution was available, but the braking situation was only now, at the track, becoming a serious problem rather than an annoyance to production model owners.

Eventually the brakes were modified by the use of larger drums with cooling fins and a tougher lining material, and they worked well enough for success at Sebring for several years, although they were undoubtedly unwieldy and heavy.

When race day came round the four Corvettes were just about ready, but their drivers were almost completely without preparation. Two cars went out early on, but the other two did better. One came fifteenth, although only one gear still worked by the end of the 12 hours, and the modified car, with clutch slip almost from the start of the race, was nursed into ninth place. Although it was hardly a clean sweep of the board it was a creditable first-time effort for two ailing machines, and Corvette's first serious racing venture captured the imagination of the public – suitably aided by an advertising campaign

that featured the dirt-streaked car at Sebring beneath a banner headline proclaiming 'The Real McCoy'.

Dr Thompson made his first SCCA outing a month later at Pebble Beach. Running as a private entrant, he too had massive backing from Detroit. He achieved an entirely satisfactory result, leading for most of the race and eventually coming second after braking problems meant that he was outbraked and passed by a Mercedes 300SL. From then on he continued to build up points in the Championship at race venues all over the United States.

Then two California hotrodders, Racer Brown and Bob D'Olivo, wrote to Chevrolet and announced that they could make Corvette even more competitive than the factory. In a typical backdoor arrangement they were 'loaned' a car by a Chevrolet dealer and as they worked it up to race trim the bills were paid by Campbell-Ewald, Chevrolet's advertising agency.

What the hotrodders established was that direct factory involvement at racetrack level could be more of a hindrance then a help. Applying basic techniques they beefed the car up in the engine and suspension departments and sent it out in the hands of Bill Pollack to the California airstrips to destroy the opposition. In SCCA events the driving was again handled by Thompson, and at both levels the result was eminently satisfactory, taking Corvette from vanquished to victor in a single season.

D'Olivo and Brown summed up their success by pointing out the difference between the proving ground and the racetrack: the latter is a more demanding arena, and although Chevrolet engineers fixed the car up so that it would run to the limits of the proving ground, the limits on the racetrack were always just a little bit further.

By the end of the 1956 season several points of great importance had been well and truly established, along with the records and the Championship win. The single most important point that came out of it was that Corvette was no longer a 'dog', a remark Karl Ludvigsen (Corvette: America's Star-Spangled Sports Car) attributes directly to Duntov himself. In fact quite the reverse was now true.

The Corvette was quite clearly on a competitive level with the best the Europeans could offer: after three years existence and one full season of competition it could give Jaguar, Mercedes, Ferrari and Porsche a run for their money. And it was something that any race team could handle, as Brown and D'Olivo had proved. You didn't need to own large amounts of Detroit real estate to make Corvettes win races. Since so much of the work that had been done in the Sebring hangars to make Corvette competitive had to be available to customers from Chevrolet dealers – at least on paper – in order for the cars to qualify as Production models, there were increasing numbers of performance parts available to help privateers do exactly that.

The knock-on effect was very clearly visible in the ever-climbing sales graph. With the price pegged at a sensible $3120 without options, Corvette was competitive at the bank-balance level as well. In addition, it came with a growing option list, which included speed packages for the engine and extra luxuries like a power-operated softtop.

Racing had made Corvette desirable, just in time. In fact it was Carroll Shelby who later said that racing had saved Corvette. and it is certainly true that nothing succeeds like success. In the automotive world that means winning races. Simply saying that Corvette is the fastest-accelerating production car built in America, which it became in 1956 (and has remained almost ever since), it not enough. It has to be seen to be true – and now it had been. Indisputably, sales had jumped, up from 1639 in 1955 to 4012 in l956 according to Chevrolet figures. Chevrolet, however, computed their sales charts by the calendar year, and figures for the 1956 model year were slightly lower. But however the figures were measured, there was no doubt at all that Corvette was heading in the right direction.

For the Corvette 1956 had been a watershed year, the moment at which its future had hung in the balance. Luck, dedication, hard work, inspiration and sheer brilliance had tipped the scales from 'break' to 'make'. Although there was no possibility whatever that its tiny production volume could be making anything like a profit for Chevrolet, it was looking better – looking like a worthwhile investment. It was generating a great deal of publicity and interest in Chevrolet's activities, there was a strong feeling that a healthy part of its charisma and growing reputation would rub off on its stablemates, and it was providing a useful and viable basis for testing engineering ideas and prototypes.

The situation was to remain the same for 1957, and some of Chevrolet's most advanced thinking surfaced first on Corvette.

During the World War II years fuel injection had established its clear supremacy over carburetion, and in the early fifties Mercedes had brought injection to the racetrack and from there into production. Chevrolet had been examining the problems for some years but had so far not arrived at a workable solution for passenger cars, nor really felt the need for urgency. The Mercedes system worked, but it was complex and expensive, and GM sought different solutions to the same problems.

Meanwhile the Corvette still had a troublesome 4bbl carburetion system, which could be set up to run under any individual conditions but not all at once, and gave an extremely lumpy idle when tuned to provide maximum power. Although the '56 Corvette had taken everybody – including its competitors - by storm and surprise, there was no point in ignoring the likelihood that Ford and others would reply with faster versions of their own V8s in 1957. In order to stay one step ahead Corvette had to go faster in 1957.

Ed Cole had by now been promoted to Chevrolet General Manager, with Harry Barr replacing him as Chief Engineer. Cole was determined that fuel injection should be available for the 1957 model year, giving Corvette its extra turn of speed and Chevrolet America's first fuel-injected production engine. He also had an interest in keeping the Chevrolet division ahead on the NASCAR circuits, and needed fuel injection for that as well. Cole and Barr proceeded to light a fire under the project, bringing Duntov into action along with John Dolza, the head of the GM engineering staff's fuel-injection team.

Duntov had begun studies in 1956 but had been held up following an accident at the proving ground which had left him with a broken vertebra in his back. He spent six months with a plaster cast encasing most of his upper body, and continued to work - standing up - on the fuel-injection project which he regarded as so vital.

Dolza had established the basics of the injection system early on, following principles laid down in aircraft engines. As the production start-up date for the 1957 model year drew ever nearer, what was eluding him was a metering system that would be financially and mechanically practical and would provide the correct fuel – air mixture in the cylinders.

Discussing the matter with him, Duntov suggested that measuring the total amount of air entering the engine might provide the answer. Holley already made a carburetor that gave a fine degree of control over distributor advance by using vacuum from the inlet venturi and this principle was adapted. It was indeed the solution Dolza had been

Below: On the grid at Ontario (now closed) in 1956, with a Thunderbird close behind.

CORVETTE

looking for, and from then on everything began to come together nicely.

The only drawback was that once it was dyno tested on the stock engine, the injection set-up, although it worked well, produced no measurable gains in power output from the engine. It has been carefully designed with new manifolds for better volumetric efficiency, used longer-reach spark plugs, thicker casting on top of the block to isolate the heat build-up, and mechanical lifters instead of hydraulic. There was even a new distributor, with contacts located over the shaft bearings for better accuracy. It was, if anything, over engineered for reliability and longevity, yet there was no power increase on the dyno.

It was only when practical testing began that the system declared itself. Although it didn't show up on the dyno, it launched the Corvette harder and faster than a carbureted equivalent by a dramatic margin. From then on there was little except refinement to be made – that and matching the system to the overbored smallblock, which now displaced 283ci.

This really was the secret weapon in the Chevrolet arsenal, and a landmark engine in its own right. With fuel injection this power plant was capable of producing one hp for each cubic inch of capacity, a figure always regarded as ideal by engineers. There is a certain amount of controversy about this, since the way the output is measured makes a difference to the answer: there is some evidence to suggest that it was the most favorable reading obtained; some that indicates that it was capable of slightly more. Whatever the truth, it was the number and the performance, Cole needed for the division and Corvette needed for the street.

The 1957 Corvettes looked the same as the 1956 cars had done. Under the skin, however, it was a different story. The fuel injection used was the Rochester Ramjet system and it achieved the production line by a tiny margin. It was offered on all Chevrolet V8 engines and on Corvettes basic unit. With hydraulic lifters and a 9.5:1 compression ratio, it gave 250hp at 5000rpm; with high-compression heads lifting the ratio to 10.5:1 and a Duntov cam, it produced the magic 283hp at 6200rpm.

Nor was that the only surprise Chevrolet had ready for their competitors. Built for them by Borg Warner was a new four-speed trans-

Above: The #3 car of Duncan, Kilborn and Jeffords, on the way to 3rd Place, Sebring, 1957.

mission with an extra ratio in between the first and second of the original three-speed manual. This was an added bonus and helped greatly when it came to laying down some acceleration times. The '57 Corvette moved off from standstill to 60mph in a blistering 5.8 seconds, and passed l00mph in 17 seconds. It did the quarter in 14 seconds, topping out at 94mph. Its top speed was an entirely satisfactory 133mph, putting it very firmly at the top of the American performance tree and seriously embarrassing the European exotics.

It was also able to deal with them on price: the base was $3427, a 10 percent rise over the previous year. The performance options, however, cost a fair sum. The four-speed transmission, available only from May onwards, was an extra $188, while the fuel-injection system added a substantial $481 to the bill.

Undoubtedly this was a significant factor in the sales figures - only 240 of the 1957 models left the factory with the Ramjet injection installed. Still fewer of these were the full-house high-compression versions: to emphasize its racing heritage and purpose these were only available minus heater.

To quell complaints about braking and handling there was another, very expensive, option available to the racer. RPO 684 was a package of heavy-duty springs, shock absorbers, sway bar, Positraction rear end and heavy-duty brakes which added $725 to the price tag. This sort of stuff was only a feasible buy for the serious racer, and that was exactly as it was intended. By ticking the right boxes on the order blank it was possible to buy a race-ready Corvette off the showroom floor, go out – and win!

And that is precisely what happened. Dr Thompson was at Sebring again in 1957, this time with a Production Corvette. He came home 12th overall, first in the B-Production class (the engine overbore had automatically moved Corvette out of C into B(and 20 laps ahead of the next car in his class, a Mercedes 300 SL. Now the boot really was on the other foot, and Thompson continued to humiliate the competition at every racetrack in America as he powered Corvette to the SCCA Championship for the second time.

The lower-rated (250hp) engine was still adequate for street use, although its statistics made less impressive reading. Its 0-60 time was a healthy 7.6 seconds and standing quarters were covered in 15.6 seconds, with top speed around 92mph. The difference was more apparent at full stretch, where the lower compression engine could find only 115mph. That in itself meant it was no slouch, however, and the 'only' is a relative term.

The year 1957, a vintage one for Corvette performance, was good for sales, too. Chevrolet figures show a continued rise in the car's popularity as sales jumped from slightly above four to almost seven thousand – 6904. It was, however, the last year that Chevrolet would be able to rely on its race program to establish Corvette potential. In 1957 the AMA announced its ban on race involvement.

THE REAL McCOY

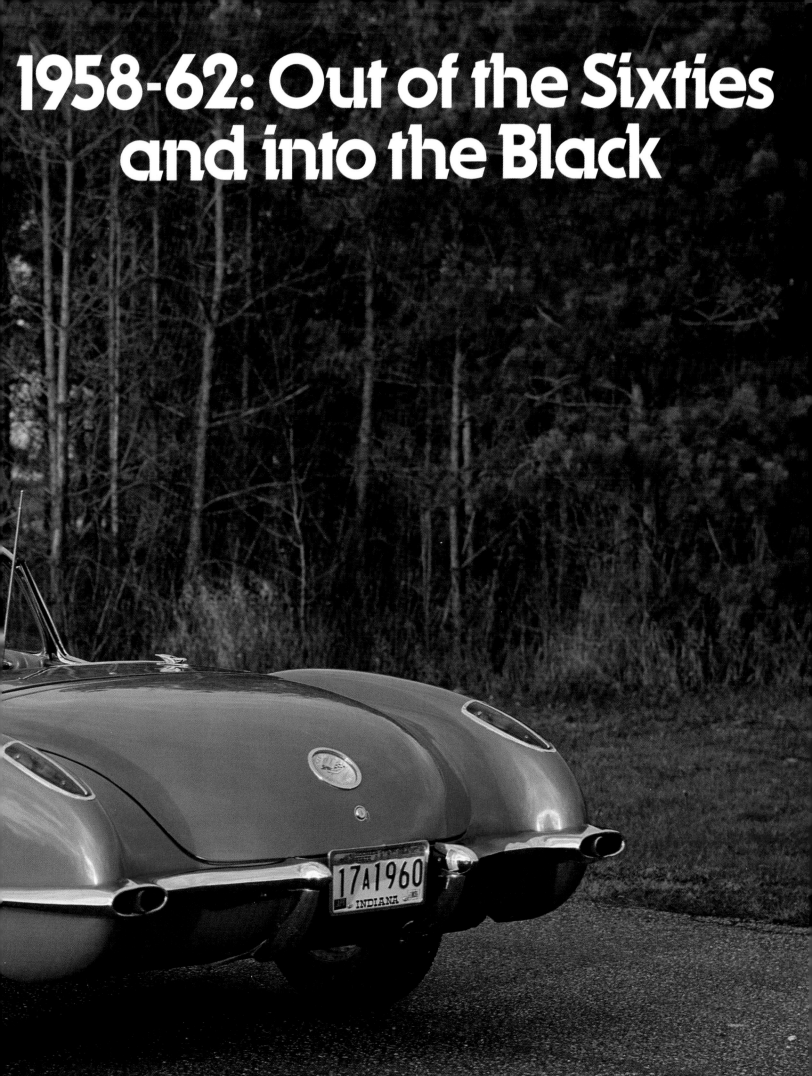

1958-62: Out of the Sixties and into the Black

By 1960 the exhaust outlets, although still exiting through the rear bodywork, were squared-off and had chrome surrounds.

The decision was announced on June 7, 1957, and the AMA Directors - including GM boss Harlow 'Red' Curtice – voted unanimously for a resolution that called on members to stop sponsorship and support for race drivers and cars. What it meant in practice was a complete ban on factory racing. In its announcement the AMA recommended that car buyers should 'evaluate cars in terms of useful power and ability to afford safe, reliable and comfortable means of transport, rather than in terms of capacity and speed'. In view of the imminent coming of the 'musclecar' era, hindsight gives these words a forlorn note of unheard appeal. And in view of the way race success had given Corvette its first real market appeal, with spin-offs across the entire Chevrolet Division, it seemed a strange way for Harlow Curtice to cast his vote.

The last race in which a factory car officially took part was the Sebring Grand Prix of Endurance in March 1958. Two Corvettes were entered and the New York Times described them as 'the first real threat to European sportscar racing supremacy'. Now, offically at least, the threat was canceled.

Unofficially it was to be a different story, at least for the next few years. At Chevrolet, Duntov had already entered his SS cars - part of the Corvette race and development program announced barely two years earlier – for Le Mans, and was dedicated to ensuring that anybody who wished to race Corvettes could either buy the ready-to-roll item off the showroom floor by ticking the right boxes on the order blank, or could buy any of the numerous racing hard parts individually, over the counter at any of Chevrolet's 6000-strong dealer network. Although Le Mans was now forbidden to him he chose not to dismantle his own 'back door' support system. He continued to make appearances at racetracks in a private capacity and Corvette continued to do well in competition.

In fact it remained the fastest domestic-built production car available in America, and in its high-compression injected form was one of

Above: The chrome-laden '58 model. It looked bigger and heavier, and that's exactly what it was.

the fastest genuine volume-built cars in the world, although not a great percentage of Corvettes was ordered in this fire-breathing version. In fact only 10 percent of the year's sales went to the 290hp fuel-injected engine, with half of that number choosing the 250hp injected unit. On the track the benefits of having that kind of performance available were evident in the results sheets. The Corvette took the SCCA Group B Production National Championship title for the year, driven by privateer Jim Jeffords. The Sebring GT Class fell to

CORVETTE

Above: By 1959 a lot of the heavyweight extras – notably the dummy hood louvers – were gone.
Left: The 1960 car was lean and elegant, the best-looking Corvette so far.

Dick Doane and Jim Rathman, and at Pike's Peak Ak Miller won the sportscar class in 15 minutes 23 seconds.

All of this was now achieved without official factory participation. The Chevrolet race program, which had always been deeply involved with individuals and dealerships, was well suited to this backdoor effort, and a great deal of planned activity continued virtually as before. In addition, it had been policy to translate race success into parts department sales; aside from other considerations, homologation regulations required that items that were developed for racing should be available over the counter, and this had always been the case. It's fair to say that although the AMA edict brought a halt to a great deal of 'high-visibility' racing - and thus also halted a large amount of Corvette development work – its impact wasn't felt too severely in certain quarters.

Meanwhile, for the industry in general, things weren't going too well. The year 1955 had seen Chevrolet riding high as America's number one seller, at 1.7 million vehicles, with Ford close behind at 1.4 million. In 1957 Ford had been top at 1.6 million, with Chevrolet running second at 1.5 million. But l958 was a depression year, and by its close the industry figures made fairly grim reading. Although back on top of the pile for the year, Chevrolet sales were just 1.1 million, and second-placed Ford's were even worse – 987,945 vehicles.

Within that framework any individual car that held its ground had done well; one that had increased its grip on the market was a winner. Two of the year's three success stories are particularly relevant.

Sales of the Thunderbird, launched with immediate success in 1955, had dipped in 1956 and come back strongly in 1957. Even so the figure for the year was only 21,380. Although that was well ahead of anything Corvette could boast, it still fell short of Ford's expectations and needs. In 1958, then, they followed their original bold step into what they had termed the 'personal car' market with another

equally brave decision. Although enthusiasts and fans saw the change from the two-seat T-bird to a four-seat convertible as a retrograde step, it was an excellent piece of marketing expertise. Ford had put their finger exactly on the pulse of another untapped market and sales in 1958 all but doubled, to 35,758 units.

The change left the American-built sportscar market with only one contender again, and Corvette was unchallenged. Calendar year sales stood at 8821 units by the close of 1958, a definite rise over the previous year, and in a seriously declining market. But even that wasn't a completely accurate reflection of the picture, for model year production was even higher at 9168 units. Calendar year production was slightly higher still, at 9298 vehicles, and for a while at least it seemed that Corvette might have broken the 10,000 barrier for the first time. Even if that particular achievement had to wait a couple of years, 1958 was notable for one other reason: it was the first time in its five-year history that Corvette showed a profit for Chevrolet and GM.

All of this was achieved without the use of race success in advertising - one place where the AMA rule was observed very strictly - and practically without mentioning performance directly. It was also achieved with what was probably the ritziest Corvette ever made, with the possible exception of the 1978 Limited Editions and pace car replicas, for 1958 had seen the arrival of a new-look Corvette, bigger and heavier than ever before.

Design work for the new car had begun as early as 1955, with inspiration from various sources as a starting point. One of them was the successful Mercedes 300SL. Its six-cylinder engine developed 215hp in fuel-injected form, and its lightweight construction, based on a spaceframe chassis, allowed it a top speed of some 165mph. It showed instant top-class ability when it began racing in 1952, and demonstrated top-class reliability as well, cruising to a win in the 1952 Le Mans 24 Hours after previous race leaders had fallen by the wayside one by one. More relevantly to the projected new-look Corvette, it was a closed coupe entered by gullwing doors, a layout that GM Styling would later be looking at very closely.

The reason for the project was the Oldsmobile entry for the 1956 Motorama. The Golden Rocket was designed and built during 1955,

---

1958-62: OUT OF THE SIXTIES AND INTO THE BLACK

and apart from its overall sleekness it, too, was a closed coupe. Entry by conventional doors was assisted by a small panel above each side window which opened upward as the door was opened. Work on the new Corvette shape progressed virtually alongside the Oldsmobile project.

The traditional body and frame construction was dropped in favor of a lighter unibody arrangement which included a change from fiberglass to a largely aluminum body. This was a closed coupe - and the basic Corvette design wouldn't really have allowed a convertible body without incurring overwhelming weight penalties when the necessary strengthening had been made. At the time sportscars were convertibles of necessity, virtually by definition. This willingness to abandon tradition can be laid almost exclusively at the door of the Mercedes 300SL.

However, this was yet another advanced design that would never make it into production thanks to the basest of reasons - money. Although Corvette itself was improving its position, the industry in general was having a rough time. The major changes required for the new design were seen as too expensive and it was shelved, although elements of it survived and eventually made it onto the production line.

Away from the work the GM design studios were doing on a brand-new car, the Chevrolet people themselves were working on a facelift for the existing Corvette. It was the financial restriction that meant that it would be this the Corvette buyers would see in 1958 instead of a complete restyle. This facelift was nothing if not extensive, and reflected the all-pervading trend toward extensive applications of 'cosmetic' chrome and flamboyant, if impractical, body styling. In addition it also employed the contemporary fashion which GM introduced across its range in 1958 and which would soon be sweeping the industry. The quad headlights introduced on the 1958 Corvette would be a hallmark of its styling for the next 25 years, even after the introduction of concealed lights in 1963.

But there were more than just headlights, and the facelift borrowed a few of the features from the now scrapped Corvette coupe and others from the SR. The coupe had featured a split grille with the central gap filled by the license plate. On the eventual '58 car those 'nostrils' remained in vestigial form as air intakes either side of the radiator grille, although they were dummies as far as the normal production cars were concerned. Dummy also were the hood louvers, which were not open but merely a number of serrations, and the air outlets built into the retained side scallops.

After several different approaches, including aluminum mesh, the grille remained as the same toothy aperture, although with fewer teeth. As far as chrome was concerned this was about the only area where the 1958 model had less than its predecessors. In fact it was the only area of any kind in which styling features were played down rather than up, although the dummy scoops which had sat on the fenders just in front of the windshield pillars were also eliminated in 1958. Presumably there were so many additions that these were simply not gaudy enough.

All pictures: The 1960 model differed only minutely from the previous year, and it becomes even harder as time goes by. The radio is missing and the shift-lever non-standard.

1958-62: OUT OF THE SIXTIES AND INTO THE BLACK

Introduced for the 1958 cars were chrome strips running along the tops of the front fenders, extending back from the chrome headlight surrounds to the base of the windshield. They were echoed by similar decorative chromework across the rear deck, although this was the only year it appeared.

Altogether the extra chromework gave Corvette the appearance of being a bigger and heavier car altogether. The original intentions, to build a small, nimble, lightweight sports-racing car, seem to have been totally forgotten, if not actually sacrificed, and the change in appearance and attitude met with widespread criticism from Corvette fans, both outside and inside Chevrolet. Certainly Duntov was no supporter of the extra hardware.

Corvette's larger appearance was not simply due to the styling changes: it had grown in bulk as it sprouted the chromework. On the same wheelbase as before, and with no increase in track, it was 200lbs heavier than the 1957 car and for the first time it weighed in at over 3000lbs. Most of the weight came from increases in actual dimensions. The 1958 cars were some 2 inches wider than before and almost 10 inches longer – and most of the extra length now hung over the front wheels.

It wasn't all cosmetics for 1958, and there were some worthwhile

changes made. Externally the bumpers, which had always been attached directly to the bodywork, were now fixed to the frame, giving better impact protection front and rear. And the interior, which had been the subject of frequent criticism in the past, was also revised. The major change was the move of the ancillary instruments from their straight-line position along the dash to the right of the driver into a tight grouping, two on either side of the central speedometer and tachometer. In the process Corvette grew an embryonic center console, another styling feature destined to remain with it for the next quarter of a century.

In the more immediate future there was the matter of Corvette's appearance for 1959 to take care of. There was still no major restyle scheduled, although since the dropping of the monocoque Corvette Coupe there were further, even more revolutionary proposals going through the Chevrolet design shops. Rumors about these would begin to surface in the automotive press during 1959. But with the bulk of GM effort and money aimed at an across-the-board restyle to counter the new Chrysler sales thrust, Corvette had to be content with minor changes to the existing shape.

This isn't to say that the alterations for the 1959 models weren't entirely worthwhile: they were. They consisted almost exclusively of

CORVETTE

Both pictures: 1961 models have the same basic shape but cleaner, cut-off rear, new grille, new 'Corvette' script, new hood emblem and body-color headlamp rim.

removing from the bodywork all the extra chromework and gimmicks which so many observers had decried on the 1958 version. Gone were the two chrome strips that had decorated the rear deck, and gone were the entirely cosmetic hood ripples designed to simulate louvers. The result was a cleaner overall appearance which went a long way to restoring the elegance of the '57 models. Minor changes to the interior - repositioning of armrests and door handles - were also well received, although the seats still came in for some criticism. And the dash layout redesigned the previous year now gained concave lenses to cut down on reflected glare; it still didn't meet with unqualified approval, but it was better.

Mechanical changes were few. In fact there was only one real change, but once again it was effective. Rear radius rods were added for the first time, and by reducing rear axle wind-up they went a long way to curing the problem of ferocious wheel hop under hard acceleration which had beset cars with the top power option. They also largely accounted for a small weight increase, up now to 3080lbs.

Under the hood there was no change, and choices remained the same, with the 290hp injected engine remaining the racers' choice and the 'cooking' 230hp carbureted engine topping the sales list. The base price was by now more than $3700, which was still very competitive and attractive. But checking off the options for a full-house performer with a touch of luxury would increase that considerably. The 290hp engine added almost $500 to the cost and basics like a heater put another $120 on top of that. The 'Wonder Bar' self-seeking radio cost another $150, although that was a luxury, as was perhaps a hardtop to complement the standard folding top, at $236. With a well-sorted option list on board the cost of a real performance Corvette could easily rise above $5000 making it an expensive item for the time.

The only compensation for this was that it did still perform rather well, easily rivaling Porsche and Jaguar and giving some of the real exotics like the $10,000-plus Ferraris a real headache. A fully loaded Corvette – and that meant having the 4.11:1 rear axle as well as the 290hp engine – could hit 60mph in about 6.5 or 6.6 seconds, depending on who was driving and which magazine road test you believe. Higher up the scale the results become more consistent, and 0-100mph times are all in the 15.5 seconds bracket. Standing quarter miles are again subjective, but 14.6/95mph is a realistic figure, as is the top speed of 130mph.

These sort of figures made it still one of the fastest cars available at the time. By comparison some of the other legendary names were little better than pedestrian when it came to the mathematics of brute power. *Motor Trend* magazine matched Corvette against a 356 Porsche and the result was a massacre for St Louis, with Stuttgart relegated to the weeds. Corvette 0-60 time showed up as 7.8 seconds, Porsche at a slothful 15.2. The Corvette was through the quarter in 15 seconds, Porsche in 19, and the GM car outhandled Porsche as well.

Even so the factory ban on racing began to bite a little more this year. Only Jim Jeffords and his 'Purple People Eater' (named after the song rather than the other way round) continued to wave the Corvette banner, once again taking the SCCA Group B National Championship. Despite an apparently low profile the 1959 Corvette was generally hailed as the best so far and was clearly a great deal different to the original. Although it had grown a lot of extra weight, of which Duntov disapproved mightily, its performance was now far closer to its original philosophy, and was being maintained at an aggressively competitive level even without the benefits of a factory race program. Someone, somewhere, was getting a great number of sums right and the bulk of this success was by now directly attributable to the guiding hand of Zora Duntov. Having arrived in the Corvette program almost by coincidence he had made it virtually his own, a truth that was not officially recognized by GM until 1968, when his status as Corvette chief engineer was confirmed in writing.

The excellence of the 1959 model was not, however, reflected in the sales figures to the same extent as it was in the magazine road tests. Calendar year production was 9088 units in 1959; model year production 9670. Both showed a slight increase on the previous year's figures but not as much as had been hoped, and certainly not as great as the growth for the whole industry. But things generally were looking up, as Chevrolet sales climbed back toward 1.5 million for the year.

With the improvement in the overall economic climate within the industry it seemed that 1960 would be a better year, and optimistic tipsters hinted heavily that 1960 would see the introduction of a radical new Corvette. It was not the first, or the last time that these advance guesses would fly wide of the mark.

The process of car development is necessarily lengthy and complex. Design work for the 1958 Corvette began in late 1955, two years before the car needed to be ready for production. That in itself is a fair guide to the speed with which the original Corvette was moved into production in 1953; two years for a restyle is rather more comparable with the average timespan normally involved in this sort of thing.

Consequently there are, within any car manufacturing plant, a number of development programs going on at any time. While most will be confined to the 'bread-and-butter' sedan car range there will always be some experimental work concerned with futuristics and/or

1958-62: OUT OF THE SIXTIES AND INTO THE BLACK

the dream cars for the styling shows. By definition the experimental work contains a great many 'maybes' and 'if onlys', which for one reason or another will never reach production. Indeed, it would be unrealistic to expect it to be otherwise.

Some dream cars eventually make it on to the street, and Corvette is a prime example of this. Most others never appear. Frequently some features will eventually filter through to the production vehicles; others will be discarded as impractical, undesirable or, more usually, too expensive. And where this kind of experimental work is conducted within an organization that already manufactures a flagship which is supposed to represent the forefront of current vehicle technology, then it is only natural that much of the development work will

The '61 still features a side panel in contrasting color as an extra-cost option and the beginnings of Bill Mitchell's styling influences, particularly at the rear.

CORVETTE

be centered around it. This is likely to be even more true if the vehicle in question is in low-volume production and can provide a suitable testbed for advanced thinking.

All of which is an excellent description of the position of Corvette within the General Motors set-up, from the moment of its inception as a dream car right up to the present day. This also accounts for the fact that Corvette has always been the center of a great amount of research and development work. This has resulted in some truly creative and advanced designs which have got closer to the production line than they might have done based around another GM car, simply because of what Corvette is and represents.

Every time it has happened the rumors have sneaked out into the press well in advance. The urgent advice to 'wait for next year and the wild new Corvette' has been virtually continual, more or less factual and has seldom come true. Nevertheless, the GM studios have produced a number of innovative and excellent vehicles, far ahead of their time, most of which still exist.

For 1959 the hot tip was the GM Q-car. scheduled to be the brand-new Corvette in 1960. It was based around a transaxle design GM were developing for the entire passenger-car range, and was planned to go into production in manual and automatic versions, with inboard brakes and even starter motor included in the package. For Corvette it represented independent rear suspension, at last, and no time was wasted in getting a Corvette design drawn up round the project.

The project was stated to include other innovations like dry-sump lubrication and concealed headlights within a sleek monocoque design with wraparound windshield glass, and was truly a radical departure, not only for Corvette but for the industry as a whole. However, the entire Q-car project was shelved, taking the new Corvette with it. Officially it was the recession in the industry that caused the demise of new projects, particularly anything as unusual as this one. Many people felt that the whole affair was little more than a smokescreen for the launch of the ill-fated Corvair – itself derived from a 1954 Motor-

1958-62: OUT OF THE SIXTIES AND INTO THE BLACK

ama dream car based around the Corvette, although by now the name was all that was retained of the original project.

But certain large chunks of the Corvette Q-car survived, eventually making their way onto production Corvettes. The wraparound split-window appeared on Bill Mitchell's 1963 Sting Ray, which was heavily based on the Q-car's sleek shape in any case. The Sting Ray also included the concealed headlights, and Duntov continued to work away at independent rear suspension for a number of years before he brought it to the production line in 1964.

What finally appeared in 1960 under the Corvette banner was virtually indistinguishable from the previous model - from the outside.

Above: '61 was the last year for the 283 V8.
Below left: The crossed flags are replaced by a 3-bar insignia on the fender.
Below right: Wheel covers are slotted to allow cooling through to the brakes.

Most of the changes were mechanical and they were almost all entirely advantageous. The heavy-duty handling package had finally succumbed to the AMA no-race edict, but had been replaced by a larger-diameter front sway bar and a brand-new sway bar at the rear, which went some way to keeping the handling up to track standards.

Under the hood came even better news: the compression ratio of the injected 283 was upped to 11:1. Together with revised and larger valves and alterations to the injection system the result boosted engine output to 315hp. Aluminum heads, later to make unhappy appearances on Vega and Monza, were a short-lived feature, their high failure rate due to their susceptibility to heat damage.

However, in 1960 Corvette reliability was put to the ultimate test and passed with a more than respectable result. Four Momo-prepared cars appeared at the Le Mans 24 Hours, three entered by Briggs Cunningham, one by the Camoradi team of Lloyd Casner. The Camoradi car was placed tenth, although it hadn't covered the minimum distance for its class and was thus officially listed DNF. But one of the Cunningham cars, shared by John Fitch and Bob Gross-man, came home in eighth place, on its first outing in the most arduous and prestigious race of its kind in the world.

In many respects 1961 was an unremarkable year for Corvette, although the styling changes again had their origin in the experimental cars that had been developed behind the scenes. Principally this involved the work of William L. 'Bill' Mitchell, who applied a gentle facelift, using as a basis for some of it his Sting Ray race car and the XP-700 show car.

The influence from these two cars was most evident at the back. The cut-off 'ducktail' featured noticeable fender bulges over the rear wheels, giving the car a leaner, 'waisted' appearance. There were dual rear lights placed at the extreme outboard edges of this flat rear.

CORVETTE

It was a general appearance that was to remain part of Corvette design right through to 1984.

Apart from being an improvement in looks, the new rear brought a 20 percent increase in luggage space as a bonus, although it didn't add to the rear overhang. In fact the 1961 Corvettes were marginally shorter than the older style and practically identical in weight. The toothy grille was dropped in favor of a cleaner-looking mesh item, and front-end appearance was tidied up even further by changing the headlight surrounds and the trim which led back from them to the base of the screen pillars from chrome to body color. Inside, the biggest single panel in Corvette's fiberglass body was redesigned around the new transmission cases and the new floor, featuring a narrower central tunnel, gave increased footroom to driver and passenger.

The engine choices remained the same, with the 315hp fuel-injected 283 remaining the top option, although even the basic car had a 0-60mph time in the high sevens, only two seconds slower. Top speeds for all but the least powerful (230hp) model were on the illegal side of 130mph. With this powerful performer Richard Thompson collected the SCCA Group B title for 1961; with stiffer springs and a larger engine he took the Group A title in 1962.

The year 1961 was the last in which the fabled 283 unit was offered in the Corvette. The following year Chevrolet - never slow to adapt racetrack lessons to Corvette production – made the hotrodders' favourite trick their own, boring out the smallblock again, this time to 327ci. At the top of the performance ladder, with 11.25:1 compression, larger valve ports and the Duntov solid-lifter cam, this meant a massive 360hp on tap at 6000rpm, making it a serious race contender in showroom stock, and rendering even the milder engine variants overpowering streetfighters.

The early criticisms about the Corvette's transmission were by now long ended. Other considerations aside, the Powerglide automatics simply couldn't handle the mighty output of the top-horsepower injection engines and had been replaced by four-speed manuals. And with the extra power for 1962 came extra braking: sintered metallic linings were offered as options for the first time this year, and it was the last year that a power-assist option was not available. It was also the last year that Corvette was available without air conditioning as an option, the last year in which Corvette had an opening trunk lid, and the first year in which a heater was standard equipment.

Styling was yet another carryover, another clean-up act designed to bridge the gap between the old and the new, which this time was definitely on the way. So the 1962 cars lost still more brightwork as the mesh grille was blacked out, the chrome trim removed from around the side scallops and the optional contrasting color infill for

Bill Mitchell

William L. 'Bill' Mitchell was one of the most powerful and influential auto designers ever. Frequently described as outspoken, Mitchell was a visionary capable of arrogance; certainly he was disinclined to compromise and became involved in frequent, heated arguments with the upper echelons of GM management.

He began his career as an illustrator with an advertising agency and in the summer of 1935 sent some of his car sketches to Harley Earl. Before the end of the year he was working at General Motors in Detroit; within six months he was head of the Cadillac design studios. After World War 11 he spent four years working for Harley Earl design before returning to GM. In 1954, Earl told Mitchell that he would succeed him as head of GM Styling Staff; Earl had already named him to Alfred Sloan and Harlow Curtice. Earl retired in 1958 and Mitchell became head of what was the most influential auto design studio in the world, responsible for the appearance of more than half of the cars (and trucks) sold in the United States.

Mitchell's involvement with Corvette had begun in its earliest days, when it was still no more than a gleam in Earl's eye, and his early auto sketches had been inspired by visits to race meetings. It was therefore no surprise that Corvette became, and remained, his favorite during his period at GM, nor that virtually his first act as head of Styling was to dig out the old SS chassis and reclothe it for racing.

This was the Sting Ray racer, of course, which Mitchell funded out of his own pocket. Although he had help from various people at GM it was never kept on the premises and never wore a Corvette or Chevrolet nameplate. It was campaigned for two years before the pressure to conform with the AMA policy became too great.

But it was the shape of this car, however, that was the basis of the 1963 Sting Ray. As Mitchell himself is first to point out, it was this shape that gave Corvette its first really strong visual identity and brought an immediate sales boom, providing the car with its first really sound financial base since its creation.

A large part of that visual strength was provided by the rear window divider, which at the time was detested by just about everybody who saw it – with one exception. Its existence is a fair indication of Mitchell's ability to put everything he'd got into a fight for his ideas and principles. Although it disappeared after only one year, Mitchell was fairly philosophical about it, by then believing that the point had been made well enough in that time.

Mitchell retired in 1977 and, sadly, died ten years later. As the auto industry is increasingly, and increasingly accurately, accused of providing nothing better than sanitized lookalikes, designers of Mitchell's stature, ability and sheer individual flair become more valuable and, unhappily, more and more of a rarity.

A new crossed-flag fender emblem appeared in 1962, and the three chrome bars were replaced by a multiple grille-effect trim. The aluminum rocker panel molding is new too.

CORVETTE

1958-62: OUT OF THE SIXTIES AND INTO THE BLACK

CORVETTE

those scallops deleted from the order blank. Even the whitewalls were changed, from a thick to a thin band.

Sales of Corvettes were climbing higher each year: 10,939 l96l cars had been sold and 14,53l '62 models left the showroom. With styling that was now essentially four, even five years old, that increase was no small achievement. Part of it was due to Semon E, 'Bunkie' Knudsen, son of 'Big Bill' Knudsen, who had made his own reputation at GM in the thirties.

Knudsen had come from Pontiac, a division which he had personally transformed from old maid into streetracer quite deliberately. Ignoring both the AMA ban and GM policy, he had put Pontiac into NASCAR racing and won at Daytona in 1957, '58 and '59. He was particularly well-connected and well-known in the automobile racing world, secretly funding the operations of various racers who were winning events and breaking records with Pontiac products, to all intents and purposes with their own money. All of which was experience that would be particularly useful in the very near future, combating nemesis in the form of Total Performance from Ford and, of course, Shelby's famous 'snakebite' cures for lackluster Ford engines.

But for the moment, Knudsen's Corvette input was restricted to the addition of a second shift at St Louis. The extra production capacity allowed sales to increase by virtually 50 percent in one year, showing clearly that there was still an enormous reserve of untapped potential available, even though Corvette was by now a confirmed money spinner for GM.

Over the past few seasons not only had styling been refined and performance increased, but build quality had continually improved. The fiberglass material had proved itself beyond doubt, and the overall fit and finish of the Corvette was a worthy backup to its looks and performance. After ten model years, nobody could dispute that Corvette was now what its designers had intended: an excellent touring and race car for all America to be proud of.

Left: The grille is now black anodized, making it 'scoopier'.
Below: 1962 was the last year for this three-spoke steering wheel.

Bill Mitchell's legendary Sting Ray appeared in 1963.

Sting Ray-Ten Years' On

Not many people can remember Major Gordon Cooper, which is by no means any denigration of the man or his achievement. Major Cooper orbited the earth 22 times in a Mercury capsule on behalf of NASA and the United States in 1963. His excursion bears in no way on the Corvette story except in as much as it serves to indicate that if 1953, the year of Corvette's birth, was a very long time ago then its tenth anniversary year was hardly that recent either. It is true to say, of course, that most of the happenings of the year are overshadowed if not entirely blotted out by the horror of John F. Kennedy's assassination in Dallas, on November 22. But there have been five Presidents since then, and one of them is now in his second term. Twenty years is a long time.

Corvette, then, was entering its tenth year of production. During its life it had already undergone considerable change which had not only altered its appearance but also its rationale. It had grown its performance engine, the smallblock V8, in 1955. It had changed shape in 1956, grown the injected 283 in 1957 and begun to put on weight as items like heaters, which had been superflous to the original ethos, were taken on board as standard equipment.

By 1962 the car had metamorphosed into a split personality. The original intentions had been for a lightweight performer that could give the imports a run for their money on the racetrack and in the bankbook. Ed Cole had planned to develop its performance and engineering on the racetrack, applying lessons learned there to the production line and then selling volume-built cars on the basis of a successful race history. All of this was in the best tradition of the sportscar and had begun to work well when the AMA announced the racing ban.

Although this didn't halt the Chevrolet race effort it certainly slowed it down, and it did check the use of race successes in advertising. Cut off from the chosen marketing avenue Corvette began to turn into something other than an all-out racer for the track, and by the end of 1962 it was a sophisticated dual-purpose machine which combined an element of comfort - and even luxury – with the blistering performance of the fastest American-built, mass-produced road car. It also demonstrated near-impeccable road manners and a comfortable ride plus a tenacious ability to cling on to tarmac at high speed.

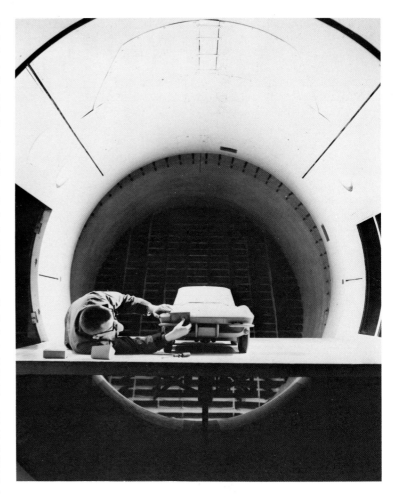

The Sting Ray's individual and even revolutionary shape underwent extensive wind tunnel testing as a detailed scale model to maximise aerodynamic efficiency.

CORVETTE

Something of a compromise, it was nevertheless an excellent car.

Despite a gentle evolution and continual refinement it had now, at the end of 1962, a body style that was essentially six or seven years old and could trace its origins, and its chassis, back for the full ten years. It had reached a peak and leveled out. Although it was still admired its arrival on the plateau had been noted and was underlined by the fact that the motoring press had been making 'scoop' announcements about its replacement for the past two years.

In Detroit, above all other places, regular renovation and replacement is an essential fact of life. Although there were any number of styling exercises and experimental projects in the works all the time, some of them certainly did relate to Corvette and almost made it into production. However, the media clamor for the new model need not have been fueled by insider information, but could just as easily have been sparked off by examination of the calendar, which would reveal that by a normal Detroit timetable Corvette's facelift was due in about 1960.

Several external factors prevented this happening, not least the general recession and a noticeable shortage of investment funds for a small-volume car like Corvette. However, the renovation could not be put off forever, particularly with people like Duntov and Mitchell anxious to keep pressing forward. And there were external pressures in this direction also, not the least of which came from Dearborn and represented yet another round in the continuing battle for market supremacy waged between Chevrolet and Ford.

Although Lee Iacocca didn't make his 'Total Performance' speech until April 1963, most of Detroit already knew what lay behind it, and had done for some time. With a new casting process Ford had developed their lightweight thinwall V8 engine, slated for the Fairlane. However, its design and build gave it most of the advantages of aluminum with none of the drawbacks: in short, it was ideally suited to race applications. This salient fact had been observed by ex-race driver Carroll Shelby, whose enforced retirement from competition had led him into the field of sportscar construction, and the new V8 was a feature of Shelby's project with AC. It promised to be a formidable combination, as well as a testbed for possible future

forays into the now lucrative and burgeoning market occupied solely by Corvette.

Chevrolet, principally through 'private' Corvette entries, had continued to be concerned with racing despite the AMA pronouncement on the subject, and it was now clear that Ford were about to follow suit. The Cobra project got under way properly in 1961, and by the time a Cobra first appeared in competition, at Riverside in late 1962, it had become a serious threat. Entered in a special category for non homologated cars, which the SCCA had established almost entirely for the benefit of the new 327-engined Corvettes, Billy Krause and a 260in Cobra led the way round and had a lead of more than a mile after an hour's racing when suspension failure forced his retirement. The point, however, had been made forcefully, and it was fortunate indeed that Chevrolet were ready with their new Corvette for 1963.

It had been a long time in the making, but when it arrived it was worth every minute of waiting. From the ground up it was a radical new departure, and the Sting Ray was without doubt the best Corvette yet.

Zora Duntov had been aiming at a new, lightweight chassis for Corvette for some time. He planned to include a number of innovations and all-round independent suspension was top of the list. For a time it seemed as if the Q-car would provide this, but its cancellation forced him into a major rethink. The limiting factor was not, of course, the ability of Chevrolet to design a successful independent rear end, but the cost of making it. Despite rising figures Corvette still had only low-volume status in Chevrolet's 1.5 million unit sales, and as always was forced to borrow the bulk of its frame, suspension and driveline components from the passenger-car production lines.

Consequently Duntov's far-sighted attempts to utilize Q-car components for a mid-engined Corvette disappeared along with the Q-car project for Chevrolet sedans. It hardly needs to be mentioned that this kind of thinking was, in 1958, way ahead of the game, nor that a mid-engined configuration is now virtually mandatory among the exoticar makers. Had Chevrolet introduced it in about 1960 on a volume-built car it would have been truly revolutionary.

Although a front-engine layout had been returned to as a basis for

CORVETTE

Left, above and above right: Chevrolet publicity shots of the Sting Ray show the controversial rear window divider which lasted only a single year in production.

the next Corvette, it was still clear that a new chassis was needed; it followed the basic principles laid down by McLean but incorporated all the knowledge gained in the interim. The center of gravity was to be as low as possible, which in turn meant that the ground clearance had to be set at the minimum possible: 5in was the chosen level. Within this the passengers were placed as close to the rear axle line as they could be, but were sat within the frame instead of above it as before. This meant that the X-member frame which had served so well for so long would have to go. It was replaced by a ladder design with crossmembers for engine, gearbox and rear axle and a kick-up over front and rear axle lines.

The engine was kept low down in the frame and moved as far back toward the passengers as could be managed. On a line of 5in ground clearance, all the main items of weight – engine, gearbox, passengers and rear axle – were kept as low as could be managed. The end result was a center of gravity at 16in above the ground as opposed to the previous 20in, and a frame with a wheelbase 4 inches shorter than before, at 98in.

This was not achieved at the expense of passenger comfort; rather the internal space was somewhat better than before. Like the few

Left: Mitchell was right. The divider stamped the Sting Ray with an identity for all time.
Below: The Sting Ray dash.

alterations to basic design that needed to be made as work progressed, this was the kind of benefit that accrued from the increasing application of Computer-Aided Design (CAD), then a relatively new technique. Although it weighed almost exactly the same as before, the new frame demonstrated a far greater torsional rigidity than the old, a factor of great importance to sportscar design and driving since this gave improved handling qualities.

Also an aid to handling was the changed weight distribution. The ideal would be a neutral 50/50; the 1962 Corvette offered 51/49, which is slightly nose-heavy. The new chassis came out at 47/53, for the first time putting the weight bias toward the rear where most drivers still prefer it. This change in balance was largely made possible by the fact that Duntov's ingenuity had triumphed over economics. He had given Corvette an excellent independent rear suspension setup while remaining inside the budget.

The IRS was effectively paid for by the front suspension arrangements, which were taken direct from the passenger-car range and installed on Corvette in slightly revised form, making substantial savings. Although this design was more sensitive to bump-steer and correct wheel alignment than before it gave worthwhile improvements in all important areas: ride, handling and steering response.

The benefits from the redesigned rear were also clearly apparent: this was the best-handling Corvette so far, and for the first time it had got rid of the endemic wheelhop that had plagued acceleration starts since the arrival of the V8 in 1955. At Sebring the new suspension, in its optional heavy-duty guise, was a whole five seconds faster than the beam axle car, a result which the experienced Corvette racer Dr Thompson described as 'astonishing'.

The improvement in handling which results from the introduction of IRS is a function not only of the ability of the rear wheels to operate independently from each other while still providing drive, but also of the big reduction in unsprung weight. The heaviest part of any rear axle is the differential, and on a beam axle this is part of the large lump of metal slung between the back wheels. The first principle of IRS is that the differential is frame-mounted and the axle relieved of the necessity to carry its weight. More savings arise from the fact that the half shafts no longer need to be encased in a metal casting, and they are in fact incorporated into the suspension system as active members, saving yet more weight.

On Corvette the driveshafts became the upper links in a parallelogram, with lower links as normal. They were joined to the differential and wheel hubs by universal joints. IRS had been fitted successfully to race cars but had always suffered from one problem. In the past, the joints at each end had been of the splined shaft type, and absorbed wheel movement by sliding backward and forward through the joint. This was a good enough arrangement, but had a tendency to lock up from time to time, especially under hard acceleration, freezing the rear suspension solid, and could not be considered reliable enough for fitment to a production car . The universal joints solved the problem admirably.

With an advanced rear end of this nature it may be normal to expect

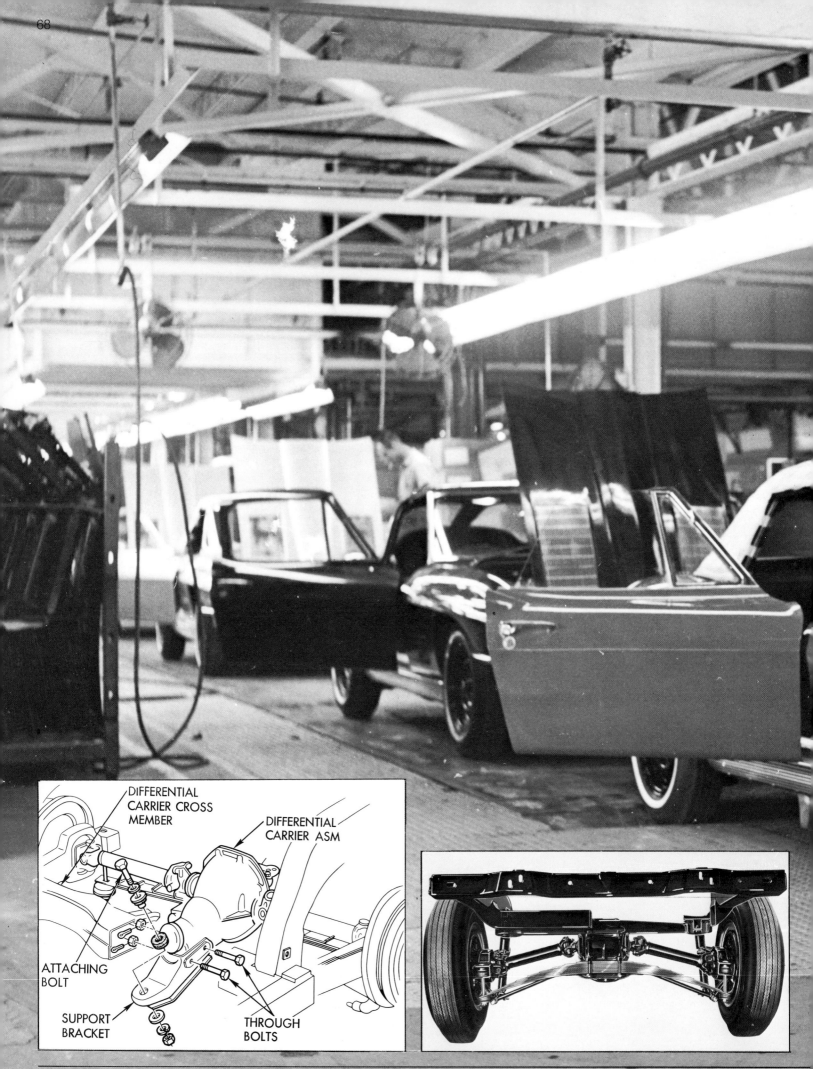

DIFFERENTIAL
CARRIER CROSS
MEMBER

DIFFERENTIAL
CARRIER ASM

ATTACHING
BOLT

SUPPORT
BRACKET

THROUGH
BOLTS

CORVETTE

As early '63 models are completed at the St Louis Plant, the drawing and cutaway show Duntov's simple and classic IRS layout.

STING RAY — TEN YEARS' ON

a coil-over-shock spring setup, but this took up a great deal of space and also cost too much. Duntov used a single transverse leaf spring, of the sort that was (and is) commonplace on agricultural vehicles but was regarded by everybody, including GM staff, as a noticeably retrograde step. But it worked very well, which is all that really mattered, and criticism of the arrangement was largely on aesthetic grounds.

The IRS produced an immediate 30 percent reduction in unsprung weight, which was a major contribution to improved handling, and extensive use of rubber bushing banished most of the traditional IRS harshness from its ride. Under the skin, the Sting Ray was a very good car indeed.

Born in 1912, William 'Bill' Mitchell was 46 years old when he stepped into the shoes of the legendary Harley Earl, who had retired in December 1958. Mitchell had been an illustrator for a New York advertising agency when Earl saw his work and tempted him to GM Art and Color in 1934. He was a keen fan of motor racing generally, and displayed a highly partisan interest in the affairs of the Corvette right from the beginning.

When the race program ended in 1957 the Corvette chassis that had been undergoing preparation for Le Mans entry was abandoned in the workshop. It had served as a testbed on a number of occasions and had been driven in different guises by Duntov himself, Stirling Moss and Juan Manuel Fangio. As an automotive curiosity alone it had some value, but Mitchell saw it in far more practical terms, as the basis of yet another race prototype - his own.

Because of the GM ban on racing this would have to be an entirely personal affair (it would end up costing Mitchell large sums of money) and the car must not look like a Corvette - or, indeed, a Chevrolet. Drawing on previous designs for the doomed Q-car a long, flattish wedge shape was designed, with an open cockpit and small windshield. From a distance or at speed it could have passed for a Jaguar D-type made from straight lines instead of french curves. To preserve

CORVETTE

Above: The classic coupe styling which has been a Corvette hallmark for over 20 years.
Left: The Sting Ray logo lasted in this form from '63 through '65.
Far left: The fuel-injected heart of the matter.
Bottom: The logo which identified the fi cars.

the anonymity of its origin it was given a new name: Sting Ray.

Mitchell would have liked to race the car himself, but the occasion simply never arose. Instead it was piloted by people long associated with circuit development of the Corvette, like Jim Jeffords and John Fitch, although it became most closely associated with high-speed dentist Dr Richard Thompson.

Elements of the Sting Ray design also made their appearance on the XP-700 show car for which Mitchell was responsible, and are perhaps also detectable in the Corvair – unluckily the first project Mitchell handled after the departure of Harley Earl. There can be no doubt at all about the lineage of the Corvette Shark show car, which made its appearance in June 1961 with a rear end all Corvette and a front end from Mitchell and stylist Larry Shinoda. And when a new body shape was needed for the new Corvette chassis due out in 1963 the Sting Ray/Shark designs, which had already provided the cutoff tail of the 1961 car, were seized upon as an ideal basis, and were adopted almost wholesale. Logical, too, was the adoption of the same name – Sting Ray.

But this was no unthinking robbery of an experimental car simply in order to provide a new skin for Corvette. While Duntov and his staff were breaking the early ground in Computer-Aided Design the design staff, under Bill Mitchell, were applying the science of aerodynamics to the Corvette body. While this is an everyday, almost mandatory practice in modern car design, it was far from being so in 1960.

Up to about 60mph, aerodynamic drag and rolling resistance are more or less equal factors. Beyond that aerodynamics play an increasingly important role in performance, stability and fuel economy, eventually becoming vital at the kind of speeds for which Corvette was designed, and of which it was easily capable. In the latter part of the fifties and early sixties this information led GM to a detailed study of aerodynamics and to the building of their own wind tunnel at the Tech Center in Warren, Michigan.

While scale models of Corvette were evaluated in the wind tunnel of the California Institute of Technology the first full-size experimental bodies were put through a series of tests at Warren. Tests on the ⅜-scale model were designed to examine not only drag but lift, side forces, pressures and airflow patterns. In order to ensure accuracy the underbody details were reproduced as exactly as possible on the models, and both engine cooling ducts and fresh air intakes were also faithfully duplicated.

Testing was extensive, and included measuring static pressure at 250 points over one side of the body. Airflow across the body was checked first by placing woolen tufts on the body surface to indicate airflow direction. These tests were closely observed and photographed. Later, small blobs of ink were placed on the body and the streaking patterns made by the airflow photographed in detail before the model was wiped clean and the test repeated with inkspots in different places.

There were four basic series of tests involved for the new Corvette, and they were nothing if not exhaustive. For each test the measurements were taken and the results photogaphed at different speeds and angles: nose up or down and at turning angles to the airstream, so that the effect of body shape could be evaluated under virtually every circumstance the roadgoing automobile would encounter.

This kind of intensive research could not provide a basic body shape, but merely refine an existing design. However, there is a maxim among engineers and designers which says roughly that whatever looks good usually turns out to be exactly that: good. Although the Sting Ray boasted an awful lot of clever engineering hidden from view, it was just that - hidden. It was the breathtaking good looks that first attracted the attention of all who saw it.

It bore no outward resemblance at all to its predecessors even though the tail was essentially a carryover. The flat cutoff with four round lights was still there, but the Sting Ray's heritage was not as apparent as it might have been – the eye was too easily distracted by the flowing slope of the rear window. The new Corvette was a coupe.

It had been mooted, almost promised, once before. Although the unibody was not there the car was still decidedly a coupe. The days of the convertible were already numbered, although it would remain as a decreasingly popular option right up to the introduction of the T-top which sealed its fate in 1968.

But the most striking feature, and the reason the coupe attracted more attention than its roadster counterpart, was the split rear window. The original design had featured a single piece of wraparound glass, but Mitchell insisted on the 'backbone'. In fact his blunt support of the divider is widely quoted as extending to a terse, 'If you take that off you might as well forget the whole thing'.

It was designed to follow the raised molding down the center of the hood (needed to clear the plenum chamber on injected engines) and provide a continuation of line, another sign that the GM styling men, at least, were convinced that the coupe would easily outstrip demand for the roadster. But while Mitchell defended it tooth and nail, he remained virtually alone. Duntov's dislike of the feature was based on the practical point that it cut down rear vision. However, its straight-line efficiency was reflected throughout the design of the new body and it was easy to see why Mitchell felt it was an integral part of the styling. The most dominant factor about the new shape was its knifelike beltline, which ran as a pronounced straight line from the cutoff line of the rear deck, round the fenders, all the way along the side and round the front, joining at a slight 'V'.

The razor-edged continuity was possible at the front because this was the first Corvette to feature concealed headlights, later to become its own hallmark but at the time a rather risky enterprise. Although they had been successful on another legendary sportscar - the Cord – their last usage had been in 1942 on a De Soto.

Above right and right: In 1964 the window divider was droped, the vents behind the door louvered.
Below left and below right: Through the front end carried into 1964 the divider was lost. By then many '63 owners had removed the divider and substituted a one-piece backlight.

STING RAY – TEN YEARS' ON

In fact the lights – or rather the retracting mechanism - proved to be something of a problem, and the Chevrolet engineers worked through five different methods of raising them before they found a two-motor system that was neither complicated nor fragile.

With a coupe bodystyle the engineers were able to build in what was described as a steel 'birdcage', and was the now commonplace side-impact and rollover protection framework built under the fiberglass skin. Its extra strength and stiffness protected passengers and allowed a reduction in the amount of fiberglass used in the body itself. The two alterations more or less canceled each other out as far as weight loss or gain was concerned, but although the new Corvette was externally smaller all over than its predecessor, it still weighed in at a fraction above the 1962 model's 3137lbs, at 3150. This can largely be accounted for by the weight of the motors and mechanism needed to raise the lights and a larger, 20-gallon, fuel tank.

Although the wheelbase was 4in less than before, the body was almost identically sized, being only marginally smaller. Front track

was half an inch narrower, rear track two inches smaller. On the sides of the body itself the curved scallops, which had extended from behind the front wheel to the trailing edge of the door, were gone, although their memory continued in two squarish, fluted air vents located on the side of the fender just behind the wheel. They were echoed in two air vents built into the pillar behind the door.

The total effect was more than just eye-catching. It was dramatic in the extreme and to most people who saw it, it represented precisely the kind of advanced engineering and design they expected from Corvette and to which nearly everyone, from Duntov on, believed Corvette had a right. The only exception to this was the almost universal dislike of the rear glass divider. Although most objections centered on the restrictions it placed on rearward vision, they were so vehement and consistent that it's hard to avoid the belief that most testers simply didn't like it on principle.

There was no shortage of custom houses and workshops who were perfectly willing to remove the divider entirely and replace the rear glass with a single sheet of Plexiglas, and a large number of buyers had this surgery performed. While this may have been eminently desirable at the time, it seems little short of criminal vandalism now. And the customizers were eventually aided and abetted in this by Chevrolet, who made a one-piece glass backlight available as a replacement part late in the model year. What the customizers

couldn't have known at the time, of course, although GM obviously did, was that the divider generated much controversy and it would not remain in production very long. A single year was all it had, and all the 1964 models had a one-piece wraparound backlight.

The fact that this was the first of the Sting Ray line, and that this distinctive feature had such a short production life, has made the 1963 Corvette the most collectible model of the entire 30 years' output, outside of the 300 built in 1953. There were, however, rather more Corvettes built in 1963 than had been the case ten years earlier. Duntov had said that the right design and engineering package – which would include IRS - would see sales of 30,000 cars. He was wrong. Styling said that sales of the coupe would eclipse those of the

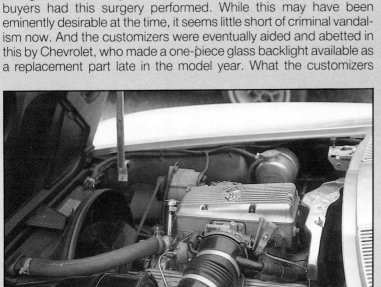

All pictures: Fuel-injected 1964 convertible. The mechanical reverse lock-out on the shift lever denotes the 4-speed version.

STING RAY TEN YEARS ON

roadster. They were wrong too. Sales of the 1963 Sting Ray did show a marked climb, however, finishing the year at 21,513 units, split almost 50/50 between roadster and coupe.

Right from the beginning the new frame had been designed to deal with a minimum of 300hp from the engine. Whatever the AMA or GM hierarchy may have had to say about it. Duntov always saw the Corvette as a machine designed to provide performance rather than anything else, and always set his sights in that direction. He felt that when compromises had to be made between ride comfort and high-speed handling, as is so frequently the case in automobile design, then it should err in the direction of top-end performance, and he set Corvette up to give its best at around 100mph. This was the speed at which he believed most drivers would want to ride it and at which they would judge it.

The drivetrain combinations for the Sting Ray remained as they had been in 1962, with the 360hp fuel injection engine as the top power option. This developed its maximum horsepower at 6000rpm, although since the previous year it had developed a massive 352lbs/ft torque capability at 4000rpm, making it an extremely gutsy automobile. Its rearward weight bias gave it a noticeable power squat on takeoff, but added to the effect of the new IRS. Times in acceleration tests were all slightly better than previously for no increase in power output: Duntov had done a good job. Aerodynamics paid off likewise, with all testers reporting measurable increases in top speed.

There was still a bewildering range of options. They included four engine choices, which declined gradually through the 340hp injection model to the 250hp cooker. Matched with this came a choice of six rear-axle ratios and three transmissions (two-speed automatic and three or four-speed manual) even before buyers began negotiations for the heavy-duty suspension and different steering ratios, which allowed them to order a car specifically set up for their requirements – and these of course might range from idling round to the nearest shopping mall to all-out drag racing. With the hot engine and axle combination, the Sting Ray had a theoretical top speed slightly in excess of 140mph; auto magazine road testers regularly turned in 135mph on tracks which were, they said, 'too short'.

Still the fastest automobile available from an American production line, and a great deal faster than almost anything available in the world, the Corvette handled better than most as well. To most sportscar fans, as well as Corvette enthusiasts, these sophisticated automobiles, with high-compression engines unrestricted by emission controls, represented the absolute pinnacle of achievement.

Yet it was far from being the most expensive of its kind, although prices were beginning the steady upward spiral which reflected its growing stature and status. The roadsters were listed with a base price of $4037, only marginally greater than the 1962 models. This is taken by many to be the prime reason for their continued sales success against the coupe, which now carried a base sticker price of $4252. Loading it with all the go-faster options brought that up by more than $1000.

Car and Driver represented the average climate of road-test reports when they said, 'The Corvette is now second to no other production sports car in roadholding and is still the most powerful'. Their assessment bore out the results of the *Los Angeles Times* three-hour event at Riverside in October of 1962. This was the event into which Shelby inserted his new Cobra, and there were four pre-production Sting Ray coupes with the full-house handling package entered as well. The Cobra retired after an hour, and three of the Corvettes dropped out as well, but Mickey Thompson brought his Sting Ray home in first place, a creditable result for its debut event.

Even in Europe, where the curiosity of the media had resulted in the arrival of one coupe for appraisal, the general level of approval was quite high – particularly when the Corvette must have seemed like the Young Pretender, threatening as it did the hard-won reputation of the domestic products. But *Motor* magazine, noted for its exhaustive and unbiased testing procedures, concluded that the Sting Ray was the fastest-accelerating vehicle they had ever tested. Their approval was qualified by matters of refinement, and some American magazines felt that quality control was not all that it could – or should – have been. But the St Louis line had been assembling the previous body for years and it can take time for a new car to assume the same familiarity to to its workforce. Early in 1962 they had begun assembling the first pilot cars which would sort out the manufacturing process and be used for initial press appraisals, and it is possible that early production-line cars on longer-term tests may have compared unfavorably with these carefully built few.

Top right: Cutaway of the new chassis and suspension.
Below: With its convertible top raised there's a trace of the contemporary Mercedes visible in the Sting Ray's lines.

CORVETTE

1963 CORVETTE CHASSIS

STING RAY – TEN YEARS' ON

The Sixties-Musclecars

In 1965 the vents in the front fender became vertical instead of horizontal, and the side exhausts were first offered.

If any one person could be said to have started it then it was Semon E. 'Bunkie' Knudsen. His virtually singlehanded attempt to resuscitate and rejuvenate Pontiac had created the legendary 'Goat' and the race for muscle was on. Although the AMA 'no-race' edict was still supposedly in force, it was clear that there was only one way to sell muscle. In fact it was the only way even to make its presence known in the first place. Accordingly Pontiac, and everybody else, took to the racetracks again, almost always through various dealerships and race teams, never in their own name.

It was Ford who really showed the whole thing up for what it was when they completed their tie-up with Shelby and announced Total Performance.

The project was launched by Lee Iacocca in a speech to the press in April 1963. Speaking of factory involvement in motor racing - any motor racing – Iacocca said that the Ford attitude was based on the belief that racing improves the breed, that anybody entering a race event using a Ford car or Ford power deserved factory support, and that Ford intended to use race success as part of its advertising campaigns, hence the 'race on Sunday, sell on Monday' slogan. Finally, Iacocca summed up: 'Our philosophy', he said, 'is based on Total Performance.'

A lot of this was very precisely phrased and was clearly in direct opposition to the wording of the AMA resolution. It was obviously not an accident, any more than it could be taken to represent the passing fancy of a single Ford executive: it was a remarkably aggressive statement of intent which followed the Ford repudiation of the resolution almost a year earlier, and in fact marked the beginning of a massive push into motorsport which finally put Ford's GT40 in the Le Mans winner's circle for three consecutive years.

With an open statement of this nature Ford were clearly planning to spare little expense to achieve whatever objectives thay had in mind at the time: this was fighting talk with backing down at some later date

clearly not an option. Faced with this GM could have responded in like fashion, could have met fire with fire; indeed, Bunkie Knudsen, now at Chevrolet from Pontiac, had privately sanctioned the building of 125 lightweight Corvettes to compete against the Cobra as long ago as the summer of 1962.

But GM management, instead of following Ford (and Chrysler shortly afterwards), had moved in completely the opposite direction, and Chairman Frederic Donner wrote a memo to his staff in the January of 1963, informing them that the company was and would remain a party to the AMA resolution, and that all unofficial racing and performance programs had to stop. Quite apart from signaling the end of a large number of ventures in various racing categories, the internal axe crushed what could have been the most devastating development program to occur at any time during Corvette's 30-year history.

Most of the people who have been closely connected with Corvette over the years have shared the same basic belief about racetrack development, a belief first scheduled to be put into practice by Ed Cole in the mid-fifties and subsequently continued by Duntov and others. Had they written their beliefs on paper then it might well have been a document very similar to the last paragraphs of Lee Iacocca's statement about Total Performance.

Duntov had been to Daytona and Pike's Peak in his experimentals; Bill Mitchell had produced his Sting Ray; and Knudsen had sanctioned and encouraged the lightweight race car that never was, the Corvette Grand Sport.

Now well into the AMA race ban, Dick Thompson became SCCA A Production Champion in 1962 *(right)*.
Below: Johnson and Morgan swap during a fast pit-stop at Sebring, 1962.

THE SIXTIES – MUSCLECARS

The FIA had altered the rules concerning GT cars, removing the upper limit on engine capacity, which was taken by all to constitute a thinly veiled invitation to American manufacturers to participate. It was largely this that had influenced Ford into its Shelby tie-up, and it was with this in mind that Knudsen okayed the Grand Sport project. Correctly handled, this was a race program that could put Corvette in line for laurels at well-known, historic race venues all over the world, including the Targa Florio and the ultimately prestigious Le Mans 24 Hours.

FIA rules required that a minimum of 100 cars had to be built to an approved, 'homologated' design inside a twelve-month period. It was decided that 125 Grand Sports should be made, 25 of which would form what amounted to the Chevrolet works team; the other 100 would be built by outside contractors between July 1962 and June 1963 and sold to whoever wanted them.

Accordingly production began on the initial five vehicles while the homologation application was still being processed by the FIA. In fact by January of 1963, halfway through the 12-month period, these cars were not complete, the next 20 were nowhere near it and work hadn't begun on the necessary 100 other vehicles. However, many manufacturers had played the homologation game before, and this apparently lax state of affairs bothered nobody at Chevrolet, although the FIA were beginning a clampdown on this sort of thing.

But before the FIA could get anywhere near clamping down, GM clamped down themselves, and the program came to a halt. That is to say that it went no further; no more cars were built and design and

Below: The 18th-placed Black/Wylie car gets tire treatment at Sebring, 1962.
Top right: Dick Thompson at speed in Puerto Rico, 1962.
Right: Very few – all too few – of these badges were fixed to the body panels they'd been made for.

CORVETTE

lightweight steel, and the whole lot was attached to a brand-new frame which was designed from scratch.

The ladder-type frame was made from tubular steel and featured side rails which were dead straight when viewed from above. This encroached into the passenger compartment, but for a race car comfort was less of a consideration than the extra strength this shape imparted. Tubular crossmembers joined the rails together at the rear and a massive tube at the front was curved upward at each end where it joined the rails. In side view these rails rose slightly at the front and incorporated a pronounced kick-up at the rear to accomodate the IRS.

The body was made from fiberglass, but the mat was hand-laid, extremely thin and very light. It was fixed to the frame at eight points and lifted off in a single piece. The rear window divider was absent – this on a design that was being laid up before the public introduction of the 1963 split-window, remember – it had fixed lights behind clear Plexiglas, saving the weight of the motors needed to rotate them, and it featured a removable rear decklid which allowed access to the spare tire.

Unlike the very basic Cobras, the Grand Sport had a fairly high level of interior trim which even included carpets. The stock instrument cluster was used, although some gauges were different and there was a 200mph speedometer. Steering was recirculating ball, similar to stock, but with a very fast, two turns from lock to lock, ratio.

The coupe body, despite all the aerodynamic research that had gone into its design, had a fairly high drag coefficient which was a function of its size and huge frontal area as much as anything else. In order to overcome this it was decided from the outset that it would need a new engine giving overwhelming horsepower, but when the first Grand Sport was completed this was not yet available, so it was fitted with a more or less stock injected engine which featured the experimental aluminum heads.

This was the car with which Duntov went to Sebring in December 1962, taking part in a tire-testing session along with various other stock and experimental vehicles, and it was here that the disk brakes

development work on the engine, which Duntov had envisioned to give it the power to outrun the Cobras, was also halted. However, there were five cars more or less finished, and halting the program didn't necessarily mean junking the completed hardware.

In the best traditions of the kind of backdoor race effort that Chevrolet had been running for some while, it was aranged that one or two favored people should 'borrow' the finished cars, and they made their way on to the racetrack despite GM policy.

The basis for the Grand Sport was the new lightweight suspension of the Sting Ray, treated to yet further weight-saving techniques. The diff housing was made from aluminum, and special rear radius arms were drilled to reduce weight still further. Replacing the vast and powerful drum brakes were new power-boosted disk brakes all round. These existing three-pot Girling items with aluminum calipers were suitable for the Grand Sport because of its lighter weight; Girling had already said that the weight and speed of the showroom cars gave this disk an unacceptable performance on the road. Front suspension was also specially fabricated, made largely from thin,

CORVETTE

Above: 1962 SCCA B Production Champion Don Yenko.
Below: Taking the flag at Sebring.

failed their first test. Heat build-up led to serious fade, and to overcome it the disks themselves were increased from half to one inch thickness. Weight increase was kept down thanks to the ventilating passages built in, and the new disks reduced temperatures by as much as 100°F during high-speed stops.

It is rumored that it was, at least in part, these tests that brought about the axing of the Grand Sport program. They had not been approved by the management and had been conducted in too public a manner for it to be possible to ignore the disregard of the AMA ban that clearly existed at certain levels within GM.

When the program was cut off, the engines were still not ready, although Duntov's design work was more or less complete. Although he was a fine all-round automotive design engineer, where Duntov really excelled was at squeezing the last drop of power from an engine. In this case it was hardly necessary since the design was virtually free from the budgetary restrictions that make miserly technique a necessity.

The base for the Grand Sport powerplant was the 327 block, specially cast in aluminum, using dry liners. With a longer stroke, its capacity could be increased to anything up to 402ci by using longer rods. The bottom end was already strong enough to cope with the task, and Duntov turned to the cylinder head. He had already created a masterpiece in the legendary Ardun conversion for the flathead Ford, and now performed similar marvels on the Chevrolet aluminum head. The trick was in the valvework, which was a sort of 'semi-hemi' arrangement which apart from other considerations, permitted the use of much larger diameter valves. Operated by pushrods, they lifted high and stayed open long, putting the engine power high up in the rev range.

Smart head design didn't stop there, and an extra spark plug was incorporated for each cylinder. Although there was only one distributor, there were two coils. A modified Rochester fuel-injection system was fitted, using individual ram pipes to each cylinder; with these and its sixteen plugs the engine even looked like a performer.

That is precisely what it was. On paper, at its maximum 402ci swept volume, using the highest (12:1) of the three alternative compression ratios, it could have delivered as much as 600hp, higher than any comparable car and certainly no bad figure for a 327 engine. Lower down, with a shorter stroke – yet longer than stock – and a 377ci capacity, the calculations showed 550hp at 6400rpm, still a fearsome capability.

Sadly, this engine was never fitted into a Corvette Grand Sport, although it was built, and there was no chance of discovering whether its hoped-for power could be realized , what kind of acceleration figures it would have produced, or to what astronomic top speed it might have propelled the 2000lb Grand Sport. When the two completed cars were 'loaned' to Dick Doane and Grady Davis they left Chevrolet via the back door (some stories still say that they left in unmarked trucks) and were fitted only with standard 360hp fuel-injection iron engines, which made it impossible for them to produce the kind of performance they had been designed for. Nevertheless, they did race, and didn't fare too badly at it.

THE SIXTIES – MUSCLECARS

CORVETTE

All pictures: 1965 Sting Ray Convertible.

THE SIXTIES — MUSCLECARS

The first outings for the Grand Sport were not exactly enormously successful, partly because there were the only-to-be-expected teething problems, partly because the drivers – and that included Dick Thompson – were deep in other race commitments and partly because the cars were forced to compete way over their heads. Although none of this would have mattered very much if they'd been fitted with the right engine, the Grand Sports were drastically underpowered without their aluminum engines.

The first outing was beset with problems. However, although he wasn't in contention for race leadership, Dick Thompson did establish that the Grand Sport was several seconds faster around Marlboro than his own Sting Ray. There followed a series of race entries that were little short of depressing, resulting in a number of class placings but no wins, until Watkins Glen in August. There a failure in the leading Chapparal let Thompson take the Grand Sport to its first victory.

Even this success was not sufficient to prevent the crowing noises emanating from the general direction of Ford and, more particularly, Shelby. While Corvette was receiving a beating on the racetracks it was also taking one on the street. Accustomed for many years to an untouchable supremacy, Corvette owners were taking as much of a real and verbal thrashing as the factory. Although it appeared that there was nothing that could be done about this after the Grand Sport program - known at GM as Operation Mongoose for some very obvious reasons – had been cut, there were still three more Grand Sport cars finished and standing idle.

While it was unthinkable that Chevrolet could have any dealings at all with motorsport it was quite within the bounds of possibility that another 'private' entrant could still help out. The outfit Chevrolet chose to assist them was run by youthful John Mecom, whose smart blue-liveried team had been doing great things in SCCA racing.

This team was lent the two cars that had already been out on the track, and a third car was 'liberated' from Warren, along with three special engines ostensibly supplied for installation in other cars Mecom already owned. Because the engine development hadn't gone the whole way before the enforced halt, the 377ci aluminum engines, with aluminum heads, were not fuel injected, but were instead given four dual-choke Weber carburetors. Instead of the planned 550hp, these power units produced a still quite healthy 485hp.

The cars were prepared after the end of the 1963 race season proper when the smug crowing from the Cobra camp was at its loudest. Painted in Mecom's blue color scheme, they were shipped to the Bahamas for the Nassau Speed Week in December. They arrived at the very end of November and, incredibly, the town was crowded with Chevrolet engineers, all of whom had decided to vacation in the same place at exactly the same time.

The first event, on December 1, was the Tourist Trophy. Well-established at the front of the grid after practice, both Grand Sports retired with trouble in the back axle. Most of the problems were associated with the newness of the axle and diff components, which hadn't been run in properly, and now the fortuitous presence of all those Chevy engineers paid off in spades. A cooling system for the rear axle oil was installed, and both cars were ready for the next event, the 112-mile Governor's Cup, for which all three Grand Sports were entered.

A Scarab-Chevrolet came first, a Ferrari second, Penske's Grand Sport was third, Pabst fourth and Thompson, running with problems, made fifth place. Behind them all, the nearest Cobra came home eighth. Then in the big race of the week, the 250-mile Nassau Trophy, trouble with hood fastenings dropped both of the Grand Sports entered from third and fourth to eighth and fourth, after frequent stops to have the hoods taped closed. The highest-placed Cobra was seventh.

The Chevrolet engineers returned from their 'vacations' in jubilant mood, having satisfied honor on behalf of themselves and Corvette owners generally. Shelby was naturally unhappy at having been trounced by what amounted to a full-house Chevrolet works racing team, and could only look forward to more of the same. Back at Warren the last two Grand Sport cars were being prepared for the high-speed Daytona event, and with this in mind were cut down to roadsters in an effort to reduce their drag figures. but although the work was finished in time the headlines that Nassau generated had

Above right: The Grand Sport cars arrive at Nassau on November 30th for the 1963 Speed Week.
Below: Cut down to a convertible to run at Daytona.

CORVETTE

acted against the project; once again Frederic Donner was forced to remind his recalcitrant racers at Chevrolet that a ban on motorsport involvement existed. Once again the project was stopped.

This time the halt was for real and the cars were sold off. They appeared in various guises and with varying degrees of success all through 1964, and in December they returned to Nassau, or at least Penske did. Alone he took on an early 427 Shelby Cobra and Ford's own GT 40 – and won all three big events, the first from another Grand Sport and the last in a Chevy-powered Chapparal.

But without Chevrolet's full backing the Grand Sport program never achieved all that it was designed to accomplish, and Chevrolet left the door open for Ford to march inexorably on to a place in motorsport history at Le Mans.

Out on the street, however, Corvette's stock was soaring again, thanks to track success at the end of 1963. By then the facelift for the 1964 cars had already been shown to the press and the most noticeable difference was that the rear window divider was finally gone. There were other small touches as well: the dummy hood louvers were also gone, and the dummy air vents on the coupe door pillar were converted to practical use. They remained a dummy item on the left, but the right-hand vent was now open and included a built-in blower motor which was designed to pull fresh air for ventilation through the car. It was not noticeably successful at this, largely because the motor was not up to the task, and it was a modification that survived for only one year.

To a large extent there was a sort of clean-up campaign around the 1964 model which was the same kind of thing that had happened in 1959 after the very showy, almost gaudy 1958. The '59 model had been so well received after the chromeplate excesses of the previous year that some people suspected it may almost have been a deliberate marketing exercise. Mitchell, however, was a believer in chrome, although not to excess, and always felt that there had to be something in a car to distract the eye. He gave in over a lot of things on the 1964 model - like the rear divider - largely because he felt that the point had been made and the Sting Ray's visual identity firmly established after just the one model year.

There were a number of mechanical refinements made as well; the two top-performing engines were given new valves and ports as well as a new camshaft to replace the Duntov grind which had served so faithfully and well since 1956. To go with it was a new four-speed manual gearbox which was light, positive and very effective. It became the necessary performance option and was listed in so many hot sheets on so many cars that it was known after the GM Plant in Indiana that made it, and inclusion of a Muncie gearbox became almost mandatory.

In this form the 327 reached its most powerful format ever; it was a street engine that delivered the same 375hp at 6200rpm and 350 lbs/ft of torque at 4600rpm as had the engines in the Grand Sport Corvettes delivered to Dick Doane and Grady Davis. It should be remembered that it was from about this time that the output figures quoted by Detroit in general started to become rather misleading. The musclecar was beginning to boom properly – and the general disapproval of the whole ethos also started to blossom. For a while big horsepower numbers were the best way to sell a car, but toward the end of the sixties the pattern was beginning to reverse, and performance and horsepower were becoming very unpopular words in the Motor City.

Chevrolet released these shots of the Sting Ray convertible to the Press in 1965.

CORVETTE

THE SIXTIES — MUSCLECARS

In the end there was an agreed total ban on horsepower advertising, and as what had once been only a possibility became more and more of a reality Detroit used the numbers less and less. In the early musclecar days they quoted the best figures they could obtain, usually taken from a blueprinted bench engine running without accessories and drivetrain. Later they moved closer to net figures, with all the ancillaries fitted and spinning, and there was often a possibility that the numbers were deliberately played down in order to avoid antagonizing the environmental lobby.

Thus Chevrolet may have been telling the truth when they said that the output of these engines was 375hp at 6200rpm, but with an engine devised to give its best at the top end, and designed with a 6500rpm redline, it could have been higher.

But although there was no doubt that it was still easily possible to order a streetfighter by checking the right engine, gearbox and axle option boxes on the order blank, the bulk of customers were ordering the more sedate versions. In fact, it was about now that equipment buying trends began slowly to swing in favor of luxury items and away from the straight performance options, so that by the end of the sixties the great majority of Corvettes were leaving St Louis with power steering and power windows, as well as air conditioning.

This was recognized and acted upon for 1964, and the two low-key engines of 250 and 300hp were fitted with hydraulic lifters, much quieter in operation than mechanicals. In fact this was, perhaps, the most significant part of the improvements for 1964 – not just the lifters, but the overall smoothness. First-year Corvettes, or first-year anything, often have a reputation for being slightly less than perfect, and in Corvette it is certainly true that the second-year of any new model has been more favorably received by press and public alike than the first-year cars.

The 1964 models had been treated to a thorough examination by teams instructed to trace and eliminate as much of the 'shake rattle and roll' from the car as possible. Small alterations and the addition of some rubber bushing here and there transformed the '64, making it

CORVETTE

Above: Dick Thompson drives the GS sneaked out to Grady Davis, Marlboro.
Below: Jim Hall takes a GS round in practice at Nassau in 1963.

They were driving the competition system, a $600-plus option which was rather harsh in operation and provided less feel and more effort than most non-competition drivers would like. In fact the only thing they were good at was stopping hard and fast.

Most people felt that a car like Corvette, which by definition was an industry leader, ought to have been at the forefront of technology, and ought by now to have disk brakes. Duntov was not unaware of the potential superiority of disks, nor that they were being increasingly widely fitted to the kind of European sportscars against which Chevrolet had deliberately pitched Corvette right from the very beginning, but the matter wasn't that simple. Corvette was quite a heavy car by European standards and it developed, in its ultimate configuration, enormous amounts of power. It would be no good producing a disk brake option that was only strong enough to hold back the 250hp cars, so it had to be developed around the 375hp versions.

During the Grand Sport project a Girling disk brake had been used, although Girling had freely admitted that it would not be suitable for the extra 1000lbs the street Corvettes carried, so a development program for an all-new brake was initiated.

GM's Delco division had been working on disk brakes since 1937, but it was 1954 before they arrived at a workable system with a floating, ventilated disk and metallic pads. An improved version of this was used on a Corvette Grand Sport at Sebring in 1962 at the same time as the Girling system was found to be lacking and the larger ventilated disk fitted to it. The results of the Delco test led Duntov to the conviction that the system would have to be power boosted, but the accountants vetoed that on cost grounds.

Delco had to do a rethink and eventually their design resembled the British pattern in most respects. At the time disk brakes were similar to drum brakes in that they utilized positive withdrawal of the pads: in other words they were retracted from contact with the disk after use. Like other auto makers GM used outside contractors as well as their own subsidiary companies, and Duntov has since said that the development of a disk which featured pads in permanent light contact with the disk itself was largely the result of work he did in conjunction with Kelsey-Hayes, and then involved testing by Delco with over 100 different lining materials before the right compound could be established. But like other companies who have been involved with development for GM since then, Kelsey-Hayes found that their efforts did not result in the expected contract to supply the part thus designed and Delco eventually supplied the disk brake components for Corvette.

The eventual design was for a radially ventilated disk of 11¾ inches diameter, operated through four pistons with those at the front being of a slightly larger diameter to give a noticeable front-end bias to the braking effect. The pads themselves could be visually checked in seconds and withdrawn from the calipers in scarcely any longer.

Chevrolet brake engineer Arnold Brown delivered a paper to the SAE on the development of the Corvette disk brakes. He said that the established brake-testing course in Virginia normally provided a test run that was more than adequate to assess the capability of any braking system to meet normal requirements for passenger cars. But he told the SAE that on this occasion, 'no significant data was obtained'. The truth was that the Corvette's new disks simply outran the mountain route, and a new and more demanding brake-abuse course had to be found simply in order to take the massively powerful disks to their limits.

Corvette testers and owners since 1965 are all familiar with the braking capability of the car, which is quite simply phenomenal. The disks haul Corvette down from its high speeds with absolutely no drama whatever. They do not fade, do not pull or snatch, require minimal pedal effort (on the boosted system) and are impressively effective. When the disks first became available on 1965 models - at no extra cost – they were so effective that *Road and Track* testers claimed they were 'boring'.

It was just as well that the disk brakes were perfected when they were, for they arrived just in time to prevent the other Chevrolet surprise for 1965 from being fatal to most owners – for 1965 was also the year of the Big Block.

an altogether more civilized car than the '63 had been, and the improvements did not go unnoticed. *Car Life* had voted the Sting Ray their award for engineering excellence the year before, the first in a string of awards for the car from a number of different sources over the next few years. In 1964 they made no award at all since they were so completely impressed with the latest Sting Ray.

Even while the accolades were pouring in (although the 1964 model strangely sold less, at 19,908 against 21,115 than the '63) the design work on its replacement was already well under way and a clay mock-up already in existence, although it would not make its public and production-line debut until the 1968 model year.

For 1965 however Corvette demonstrated the few cosmetic alterations that were part of the Detroit scene and said that no model will look like last year's outside, even if it is identical under the skin. It was in this year that the last remaining vestiges of the phony hood louvers disappeared, and the side gills behind the front wheels were replaced by three upright and functional slots which exhausted air from the engine compartment.

But the changes weren't simply cosmetic. There was a new engine option which was a hydraulic camshaft version of the 360hp fuel-injected powerplant, except that it now had a single four-barrel Holley carburetor and delivered 350hp. It combined the killing performance of the big-output engine with the quieter and more refined operation of hydraulic lifters, and the demand for it was a reflection of those gradually changing trends.

Other signs of change were the demands for improvement in the braking department. There was nothing wrong with the performance of Corvette's massive drum brakes - quite the reverse, in fact. Only the year before Car Life had extolled their virtues, saying unequivocally that they were 'better by far than anything we have ever tested'.

The 1966 Sting Ray hardtop; about half of the year's production was so equipped.

The Big Block Years and the New Shape

The musclecar theory was fairly straightforward. Take a large engine and put it under the hood of a small car. Make minimal alterations to the suspension setup and fewer still to the braking system. Then make all the desirable bits, such as real brakes, handling package and so on, into options. Then although it was entirely possible for a car buyer to order himself a full-house firebreather which steamed off the line and managed to stop or corner when needed, it was equally possible for him to order a kind of uncontrollable four-wheel attack missile, rather like an Exocet without the guidance systems.

The shattering acceleration of these cars was constantly increasing and could make them as potent as Corvette. Sportscars are meant to be faster than sedans, and it was thus necessary to ensure that the two-seater stayed ahead of the game. The 375hp version of the injected 327 engine was the ultimate development that could be expected from it, but there were now street engines – like the Hemi Cuda – that were producing in excess of 400hp in big-block V8 form. If Corvette was to keep its lead then the only answer was a bigger engine, there being no substitute for cubic inches.

This was a route that Duntov had previously rejected on the grounds of the weight penalty. Corvette's finely balanced handling would be considerably upset by the extra ironwork up front – there would have to be a way to carry about another 150lbs in front of the firewall. On the other hand, the frame had been designed to cope adequately with more power than the smallblock could deliver, and everybody at Corvette was in favor of almost anything that would make the car go faster.

Chevrolet already had their own big-block powerplant for passenger cars, designated as the 'W' engine, but Corvette escaped the traditional musclecar fate of having this engine simply thrust upon it. Instead, Corvette waited two years for a street version of the 427 V8,

Above left: One of the American International Racing entries at Daytona, 1968. The team was sponsored by James Garner.
Below: The 1966 Corvette. Exhausts still exit through the bodywork, and the wheel covers, though changed, still feature the three-spoke spinner.

CORVETTE

which was another of Bunkie Knudsen's pet projects, and which Chevrolet had unveiled for stock-car racing at Daytona in 1963. The real trick part of this engine was the clever head work, which allowed good breathing through carefully shaped ports, with the rest of the head – and the valvework especially – designed around them. It was the resulting disordered array of valve stems poking through this head (rather than in formal ranks as is more normal) that earned it the title of the 'porcupine head' engine. And legend has it that because porcupines are only a kind of spiky rodent the name was taken one step further, and the engine became known as the 'rat' motor.

Strictly speaking the engine was rather more prosaically known at Chevrolet as the Mark IV, and was one of a whole family of four engines marketed as the Turbo Jet. These eventually replaced the existing big-block engine – the 409 'W' – completely.

As was so often the case, it was the racers and hotrodders who tried things out first, and Mickey Thompson had installed one of these engines in a Corvette in 1962. However, what finally emerged in street trim in 1965 was slightly different. Like other manufacturers Chevrolet had a policy of restricting the maximum capacity of an engine for installation in each size of car. For intermediates, which is how Corvette was classified, that limit was 400ci, so what replaced the 365hp smallblock as Corvette's most powerful carbureted engine was a 396ci version.

The carburetor was a single four-barrel, and with an 11:1 compression ratio it produced a quoted 425hp. Although it did add a little weight to the car (almost exactly 150lbs) and altered the weight balance to 51/49, making it slightly nose-heavy, the 396 was exactly what was required for performance, and most testers found that it affected the car's handling less than might have been expected. In fact, with new tires for the 1965 model year, some testers found that ride and steering response were better than before.

This was in large measure due to the fact that the big-block wasn't simply shoehorned in, although it was a tight fit. But when this engine was specified the car also received suspension modifications designed to counterbalance its extra weight, plus stronger drive shafts, made from a higher quality steel, to handle the extra power.

In order to squeeze the bigger engine in, the restrained, almost discreet hood bulge had to be enlarged considerably, giving the car a noticeably tougher front-on appearance. To match this it also gained some less-than-discreet side exhausts. These had appeared in muted form on one or two show cars in the past and were inspired by the Bertone design for the Iso Grifo. They had made a tremendous impact at GM Styling, and the extent of the general desire to fit them to a production Corvette can be gauged by the length of time spent getting their design right. Ellis 'Jim' Premo (who had replaced Harry Barr as Chevrolet's chief engineer) spent hours and hours on the project himself.

When they were fitted they still became hot enough to burn the unwary leg, despite the length of time spent on perfecting the insulation arrangements. They sounded tough, though, largely because their capacity as mufflers was strictly limited. Despite the universal approval they gained at the time, stricter Federal and State regulations on emission control eventually saw them phased out in 1970. Looking back it seems no bad thing that they were stopped, since they appear to contemporary eyes to be quite the nastiest design element ever incorporated into any Corvette.

For Corvette 1965 was the best year so far: 26,171 were sold, convertibles outselling the coupe almost double. This trend would reverse after the introduction of the T-top in 1968, and from then on demand for the ragtop would decline, until it stopped altogether at the end of 1973. Part of the problem was more regulations concerning impact resistance, and considerations of straightforward handling, which added more and more weight (and cost) to the convertible.

Cost was the deciding factor in the demise of fuel injection, stopped after 1965 and not to reappear again until 1973. The option list showed that the injection system added more than $500 to Corvette's price in 1965, while the big-block engine (which delivered an extra 50hp over the most powerful fuel-injected engine) added only $300. This was a slightly misleading comparison, mostly because GM's price to the customer for fuel injection was way above what it was costing them from their own Rochester subsidiary. Rochester

were less than happy, obviously enough, but GM has always taken refuge in its own vast size and felt free to treat its suppliers in a fairly high-handed fashion.

But it was quite true to say that the mid-sixties were in any case not a period in which the American automobile was noted for enormous subtlety, and big-inch engines were the order of the day. To meet this need the big-block unit was the top-of-the-range option in a revised engine chart which now included only two fairly low-powered 327 options and two big-block powerplants. Despite the restrictions on engine sizes for intermediates, this was now offered in Corvette in its original 427ci format, with 30 inches of cast iron missing.

The extra capacity – 'to save weight', Duntov told Karl Ludvigsen, claiming that 30ci of cast iron weighed a considerable amount – made a remarkable difference to the engine's power and to its performance. But despite the trend toward larger engines and more power, the anti-horsepower lobby was gathering strength. Chevrolet announced the 427 as a 425hp powerplant, which may have been quite correct. But there were a number of observers who felt that this was a conservative figure and that a minimum of 450hp would have been closer to the truth.

Their guesses were backed up by the performance figures which various magazine testers obtained. *Road and Track* did 0-60 in 5.7 seconds and ran the quarter in 14 seconds at just over 100mph. With a higher final drive ratio, *Car and Driver* made 0-60 in 5.4 seconds, and saw the quarter mile dissolve in 12.8 seconds, topping out at 112mph. And *Sports Car Graphic*, with yet another rear-end ratio, managed 0-60 in an almost unbelievable 4.8 seconds, getting up to 100mph in 11.2, although the ratio was beginning to work against it

CORVETTE

by then, eventually holding it down to a top speed of 140mph. With other ratios, the top speed of the Muncie-equipped 427 came out at over 150mph.

There was simply nothing available in America that could touch that sort of performance other than the new 427 Cobras. Only a few hundred of those were made in total, however, and the few that were in existence were reserved almost exclusively for racetrack activities. On the street, Corvette was supreme.

Suspension modifications again accompanied the big-inch engines, including stiffer springs and larger-diameter sway bars. And although on the track the Cobras were more agile than the Corvette, there were a number of options for what Chevrolet euphemistically described as 'off-road' applications which were designed to keep the Sting Ray competitive. These included even stiffer springing, a stronger, torquier gearbox and heavy-duty brakes.

Specifying the lower-output engines made the brand-new Saginaw three-speed transmission available. This was extended the following year to include the low-output big-block engine, making the Muncie four-speed mandatory only on the hottest option.

Minor changes to the styling of the 1966 models reflected the growing belief that the new body style was on the way. In fact it had been a clay some years earlier and had been patrolling around in the guise of the Mako Shark for some time; it was scheduled to appear in 1967. So far no Corvette restyle had appeared in the year it was expected, and this was to be no exception. Wind-tunnel testing had shown up some design areas that still needed work, and rather than bring out a bad car on time Chevrolet chose to bring out a better one late. Perhaps it was this knowledge of what was around the corner that kept Corvette sales down during 1966 and 1967: after the big

All pictures: 1966 Sting Ray coupe. The new hood with air inlet, first seen late 1965 to accommodate the 396 big block, was fitted throughout. The distinct 'lip' at the tail is also clearly visible.

THE BIG BLOCK YEARS AND THE NEW SHAPE

high of 1965 they dropped to 24,754 in 1966 and down again to 23,475 for 1967.

But the sales slump was by no means an indictment of the 1967 car. In fact the opposite was true, and it was yet another Corvette that was hailed by contemporary testers as a 'best ever'. The styling had been cleaned up all round, and at last there was nothing phony anywhere on the car: no vents, no scoops, no louvers. The three working extractor vents on the side of the front fenders were now five shorter (and working) slots, and the whole thing could be summed up in one word: clean.

Road and Track tested it and said that 'it finally looks the way we thought it should have in the first place'.

There were new engine options for 1967 as well. The smallblock variants continued unchanged, and the base big-block marched on without alteration. The next rung up the ladder was the 400hp version, which now ran three two-barrel Holleys, and these also decorated the top of a new big-block unit with 11:1 compression, solid lifters and electronic ignition.

The hot news, however, was the incredible L88 engine. Sadly only a handful of these were built and only a couple of them still survive. They had aluminum heads, ran a 12.5:1 compression ratio, an extremely wild camshaft and a single 850 Holley carb. This powerhouse was rated at an amazing 560hp (although not by Chevrolet, which maintained a tight-lipped silence on the subject), shoveled the Sting Ray from standstill to 60mph in under five seconds and drove it through the standing quarter in less than 13 seconds.

Only available with the complete set of racing options – including deletion of heater and defogger – this was intended solely for track use and was aimed at getting Corvettes a little closer to the Cobras in SCCA competition, although even this monster powerpack couldn't quite succeed.

It picked up a few trophies here and there, however, and although the engine fell apart at half distance, it recorded over 170mph along

the Mulsanne straight at the Le Mans 24 Hours and placed tenth overall, and first in class at Sebring, despite going out before the end of the race with brake failure.

The Sting Ray had appeared in 1963 and stayed until the end of 1967; it was the shortest-lived body style in Corvette's history but arguably the one that made the biggest impression, not only on America, but all around the world. But even with that under its belt its future as America's premier sportscar was under threat from all sides, even from within General Motors.

There was no question that the trouble lay with the accountants this time, for Corvette was selling over 20,000 units a year with no problems whatever and tooling costs for the new model would have been amortized within the first year.

Ford had followed Corvette into the sportscar market with the T-bird, and moved out again shortly afterward. Now, in response to demands for a car to do what the Thunderbird should have done, Ford had moved again, producing the automotive success story of the decade with their Mustang. In launching this four-seater they created the Ponycar, which was not quite the no-compromises sportscar that Corvette and the original Thunderbird were, nor was it the complete move to the luxury four-seater which the T-bird had become.

It was powerful and fast and dramatically good-looking, and had been growing faster each model year. The tie-up with Shelby had created the GT 350 and would lead to the GT 500. Ford were advancing on two fronts, one in direct competition with Corvette and

Below: The 1967 models looked very neat. New fender vents, the fender emblems dropped (the vents behind the doors in the quarter panels were dropped in 1966) and a new hood for the 427 big-block cars.
Above right: Jerry Thompson and Tony De Lorenzo, Daytona, February 1968.

CORVETTE

one into a new market they had created themselves. GM needed to compete directly against the Mustang, but like the rest of the industry they were left behind at the starting gate.

Eventually they had produced Camaro out of their corporate hat and were about to follow the act with Pontiac's equivalent, the Firebird. John DeLorean was in charge at Pontiac, and he wanted his Mustang-basher to be different in every respect from Chevrolet's Camaro. The initial designs Pontiac produced for the Firebird looked like nothing so much as the restyled Corvette that had just missed the 1967 model year.

Corporate decisions squashed that, and eventually Pontiac had to settle for a Camaro lookalike. GM were not alone in chasing Ford, and from 1965 onward Corvette was continually looking over its shoulder at a whole series of Young Pretenders, all of whom nursed their own ambitions for the throne, and some of whom were actually in the family. In 1966 Chevrolet announced the Z28 option for Camaro, an engine and handling package aimed directly, and very successfully, at the SCCA 5-liter Trans Am class, and their advertising drew attention to the similarity between the performance and handling of the Z28 and Corvette.

Under that kind of pressure Corvette had to do something fairly radical to keep its lead; fortunately radical new engineering ideas were not something Duntov and his team were noticeably short of – it was getting them into production that was altogether another matter.

The Corvair program had been killed off when Pete Estes took over as Chevrolet general manager, but the thinking that could have made it a winner remained (in fact it had been largely transformed into a good car by the time it was axed, but by then its reputation was unalterably all bad). Italian thinking had established that the mid-engined layout was quite simply the best for sportscar handling, but early Corvette experimentals with a rear-mounted V8 engine had demonstrated some reasonably suicidal tendencies. Later work on designs from Duntov's engineering group proved more practical, and Mitchell even began work on styling exercises for the all-new Corvette. Once again it was the tooling costs – especially the transaxle – that

THE BIG BLOCK YEARS AND THE NEW SHAPE

meant that this mid-engined layout would go the same way as the ill-fated Q-car.

Once again the 'standby' design was called into play, and this was a possible production model drawn mostly from the Shark show car, a dramatic styling exercise based around the existing Sting Ray chassis. This originally featured the Shark's tapered rear treatment, but was later refined to include the now-famous sugar-scoop rear, complete with removable backlight, which had featured on some of the early models made to go with the now-defunct mid-engined Corvette. Those models, too, had featured the clip-off roof that would appear as a T-top on the production Corvette of 1968, giving a similar open-or-closed appeal to the Porsche Targas.

This was the style that was eventually accepted for 1967. It was scheduled to appear in the same year as the new versions of the big-block, and the theory was that the new shape, plus the more powerful engines, would distract attention from the fact that underneath, the chassis was still the same.

However, the theory didn't pay off in practice: Duntov did not want to go into production for 1967 with the aerodynamics as they existed on the new shape. Testing on this had been going on since 1965, and the answers were still not right, so the restyle was delayed by a year, although the new engines went into production on schedule in 1967.

The aerodynamic problems had been largely overcome by the time the new body was due to go into production, but achieving this had led to the addition of various extra bits all over the car and had left it with vision problems both front and rear; it was to sort this out rather

than solve the overall aerodynamic problems that Duntov persuaded Pete Estes to delay its introduction for another year.

Testing had been less concerned with straight aerodynamic drag than with the tendency of front and rear to lift at speed. Duntov always carried out his investigations of Corvette performance and handling at high speed, since he believed that Corvette owners had a right to expect their cars to deliver their best at speeds over 100mph.

The lifting tests were conducted at 120mph, and it was immediately apparent that the new spoiler on the rear decklid was most effective. At that speed the rear didn't sit up at all as it did on the existing Sting Ray; in fact the spoiler kept it pressed slightly downward. Satisfactory though that may have been on its own, it also had the unfortunate effect of slightly raising the nose, increasing its angle of attack and helping to lift it dramatically, by almost three inches at 120mph.

CORVETTE

All pictures: The 1967 427 big-block. Its presence is announced by emblems on the hood (plus that new shape hood, unique to 1967) as well as the lettering on the air cleaner.

THE BIG BLOCK YEARS AND THE NEW SHAPE

CORVETTE

Left: The 'sugar-scoop' rear aspect, first seen in production in 1968.
Below left: Still with trace elements of the Sting Ray, this was the Mitchell/Shinoda replacement, 1968.

In practical terms this increased the car's drag factor by substantial amounts. It meant that the new body shape required no less than 210hp delivered to the wheels in order to maintain a speed of 120mph, whereas the existing shape required only 155hp. Without heading back to the drafting board for a complete restyle, it was evident that some modifications would have to be made to the body in order to reduce this to an acceptable level.

At this juncture a little more of the Chevrolet race involvement – backdoor and otherwise – paid dividends, since they had gained a great deal of aerodynamic expertise from involvement with the Chapparal race team. It was on this fund of knowledge that they drew, and incorporated into the new body shape a number of techniques that had already been proved in anger.

To begin with, the area inside the front fender wells was vented to prevent a build-up of pressure and allow a flow of air. On its own this measure dropped the nose half an inch and reduced the power requirement to 175hp. The nose spoiler which had been successful on the Chapparal cars was applied to Corvette, and this reduced front-end lift to a modest half inch and had an even more dramatic effect on the power requirement, reducing it to only 105hp. Even with these modifications Duntov remained unhappy with the new shape, and it was returned to Larry Shinoda for futher massage while the rest of the world waited another year for the new Corvette.

The styling studio cut down the line of the front fenders – which even so still appear impressively tall to anybody seated inside the car, although they do provide a guideline to aim with – and lowered the height of the decklid spoiler so the driver could see over it. Small alterations to the line of the rear fenders and roof helped rearward vision still further, while the front spoiler was reduced to a vestigial lip which ran right round the front and blended into the curve of the front fender. To compensate for this reduction the vents in the front fenders were enlarged slightly.

The one-piece clip-off roof was gradually abandoned, as it presented too many structural and engineering problems. Instead the two-piece roof with central divider became the much-loved T-top, which remained with the car until the one-piece clip-off roof returned for 1984.

Other features that did stay, and came directly from the Shark show car, included the use of fiber optic instrumentation in a package that monitored the function of the vehicle lighting system. Although this technique is commonplace nowadays, and is even available as an aftermarket kit, it was a fairly revolutionary step in the far-off days of the blessed 1968.

The windshield wipers were hidden from view beneath a flip-up panel which was vacuum operated. This was principally a styling feature, a direct carryover from the Shark, and many testers found it was simply a gadget, just a piece of gimmickry added on for the sake of it. Later models would have wipers which parked beneath the level of the hood, remaining just as neatly out of sight, so the critics may have had a point.

The vacuum motor was in vogue this year, although its second application was to far more practical effect. Using the technique perfected by Oldsmobile the year before, the Corvette's concealed headlights were now raised by vacuum instead of by the cumbersome electric motors, giving an added benefit in simplified switching. Corvette used vacuum to raise the lights; other makers, like Lotus, later used vacuum reservoirs built into the chassis in order to keep the headlights down. Failure of the vacuum system therefore meant that the lights would rise into the fail-safe position. Corvette was provided with a dashboard control to carry out this operation manually in the event of failure.

Before the new car was completely ready, and long before it was shown to the press, Duntov found that the parked headlamps and the

John DeLorean

When John DeLorean left GM in 1973 he was turning his back on the virtual certainty of becoming Chairman eventually. Already vice-president of the $25 million-a-year Car and Truck operation, one of the highest-paid executives in the world and certainly Detroit's fastest-rising star, DeLorean was all the more remarkable in that he stood out of the somber-suited ranks of the GM managers on more counts than ability. DeLorean was what you might call a 'visible personality'. He dressed flamboyantly, wore his hair long, associated with media people and pop stars and generally behaved in a manner certain to disqualify anyone from promotion within the highly conservative GM hierarchy – yet he was heading for the top at a meteoric rate.

As an engineer from Detroit's east side, he'd joined GM's Pontiac division in late 1956, and found himself under the benevolent tutelage of Bunkie Knudsen, then in the process of reviving the flagging 'Auntie' Pontiac by completely reversing its old maid image. Knudsen was the man who set the Detroit of the sixties alight with the musclecar. He spotted the youth market for what it was and in response produced the GTO in 1964.

Shortly after Knudsen's departure to higher things within GM, DeLorean became head of the division and a GM Vice president. He continued the sporting image, continued the dramatic rise in the division's fortunes which Knudsen had begun, and established his reputation as a top-notch manager with a flair for getting results. In 1969 his rise continued when he was promoted again, this time to general manager of Chevrolet.

What wasn't realized at the time was that one of the big reasons for DeLorean getting this plum post was that it was no longer such a plum. In fact, Chevrolet was fast becoming a rotten apple and was heading towards massive, continuing losses. DeLorean's job was to pull the division out of the mire and turn the red ink black. Considering the extent of the trouble the speed of the reversal was unbelievably dramatic: within three years Chevrolet set an all-time sales record for the industry and improved it the following year. Along with turnover, they also achieved the other half of the equation, and began making the sort of profits that operations of that size ought to make.

The turnaround was achieved mainly thanks to rigorous application of stringent management controls over divisional activity, and equally strict interpretation of the word that brought the cutback of Corvette. DeLorean rationalized Corvette virtually out of all recognition. He also improved profitability and, more importantly, production-line quality. His program of post-build inspections and quality-control systems throughout the division gave Corvette the solid reputation that saw it through the seventies. Although he didn't always see eye to eye with Corvette enthusiasts like Duntov and Mitchell, DeLorean was just what Corvette needed – a professional car maker.

central front license plate restricted airflow through the engine compartment, creating cooling problems which were especially noticeable on the big-block cars. Before he could tackle the problem fully he suffered a long illness which left him in hospital for several months.

When he returned he had only a few weeks to prepare cars for their press debut and had to solve this cooling problem in a hurry. He did it by cutting extra vent holes just ahead of the spoiler, adding depth to the spoiler itself to help force air up through the holes, and then sealing round the edges of the radiator to make sure that the air went through the matrix and not round it. The modifications just about did the trick, and were incorporated into production cars, but the big-inch versions still ran hot and are still prone to overheating problems.

Although the overheating problem had been cured, the 1968 Corvettes were not very well received. Aside from the fact that the ex-Shark gadgetry seemed to distract test drivers, there was no doubt that the curvy new shape was achieved at the cost of interior room and smaller trunk space – to which there was still no outside access. The location of the ancillary gauges in the center console was also heavily criticized, and many people complained that ventilation was inadequate.

Engines were carried over from the year before – all the surprises had been sprung in a year when there was no new body to go with them – and although they produced good times in the new shape, with top speed of the firebreather going up above 150mph, and although the new model could out-slalom the old one, lateral going up from .75 to .84, its ride was criticized in any case.

Many of the improvements in handling had been bought at the expense of a quiet ride, in the eternal compromise that has beset automobile design since the very beginning, and this was a deliberate choice by Corvette's engineers. In particular the contributory factors were the slightly stiffer springs and wider (7 inches) wheels which had produced the most noticeable improvements in handling.

The fact was that Corvette buyers were moving more and more toward the kind of luxurious and eye-catching 'personal car' the Thunderbird had become all those years ago. More and more were specifying factory air, power steering, power brakes and the more sedate engine options. In doing so they were not prepared to put up with the penalties that necessarily accompanied the handling ability needed from the driver who expected to drive his car in earnest – for whom it was still precisely tailored. Although the gas crisis hadn't yet arrived to occasion the last rites, the performance fans were already a shrinking minority.

And even among that minority there were plenty who were unhappy with the new Corvette. Dramatic looks notwithstanding, there was plenty to complain about, and the problems were centered on quality control. In fact *Car and Driver*, notably enthusiastic in the sportscar department, refused point blank to road-test the 1968 that was delivered to them on the grounds that it was 'unfit'.

Their complaints were strictly about quality control, and they cited crooked and ill-fitting body panels all round, together with leaks from the T-top and a host of other minor problems which taken individually weren't that bad, but which when added together spelled DOG once more.

The shame was that they were not alone in getting a 'Friday car', and altogether too many people were in the same position. So many complaints were made that the 1968 models now have the worst reputation of any Corvettes built during the make's thirty-year history, even taking into account the fact that it was a first year for a new style.

Despite the fact that production had been delayed by a whole year, Duntov's lengthy illness – and the subsequent shuffling about in the

CORVETTE

Below: Chevrolet publicity material made the most of the new car's dramatic good looks. Later paintwork additions *(above)* produce mixed feelings.

THE BIG BLOCK YEARS AND THE NEW SHAPE

CORVETTE

top management echelons which had altered his personal status considerably, effectively removing him from control over Corvette – meant that he hadn't been able to give the car anything like his whole attention.

It was, too, a much more complex car now than it had been at any time before. On top of the wiper flaps and fiber optics, Corvette now had more options than ever before. Besides the luxury choices of power windows and so on there was also still a massive array of different driveline components which could be selected on a mix 'n' match basis to create a car suited to very specific individual needs.

The legendary L88 option was still available, and beneath that was the streetgoing 435hp 427 with three two-barrel Holleys. In that guise, with the Muncie box and 3.55:1 rear end it ran up to 60mph in around 6 seconds, managed respectable quarter-mile times at about 14 seconds and 100mph, and had nice, long, 150mph legs. Which was not a bad set of numbers, in view of the fact that it had just put on a few extra pounds and a lot of extra inches. Although the chassis had remained the same, it had grown from 175 to 182 inches in length. Its width was virtually identical, and it was actually 2 inches lower than the Sting Ray, and weighed almost 100lbs more, at 3425lbs.

In addition to the high-output engine which could propel what was now quite a large car to those speeds, there were two other 427 engines available, at 400 and 390hp – the difference being refinement rather than power – plus a 300hp and a 350hp version of the 327 smallblock. The Muncie was still a mandatory option with the 435hp big-block, and there were two other manual gearboxes and a three-speed automatic transmission to choose from, along with six different axle ratios which could be ordered: and that was without the 'off-road' equipment which was still available for serious racers.

Then there was its new appearance, which was dramatic whichever way you looked at it. Corvette was quite a car, but somehow all the annoying production-line faults managed to obscure the view of people who saw it, and the general reaction to it was, at best, so-so. It would not be until the 1969 models appeared, minus niggles, that observers began to appreciate the excellence of its design and the elegance of its lines; it was blessed with an aggressive grace that made it one of the best-looking sportscars ever produced.

All pictures: The 1968 models were completely new. The revised interior was to remain largely unchanged until 1984. The fender vents from the Sting Ray remained, but for 1968 alone the name was missing from its rightful place (*below*).

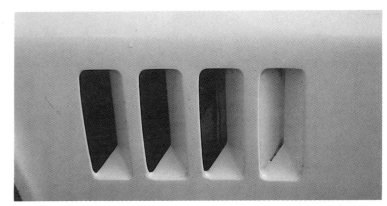

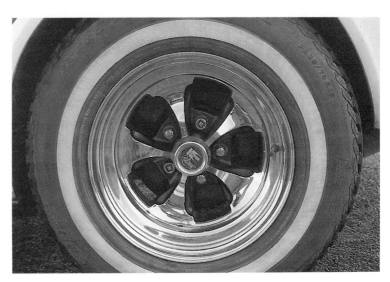

THE BIG BLOCK YEARS AND THE NEW SHAPE

Heraldry on the street.

CORVETTE

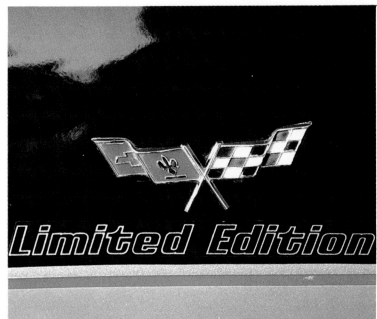

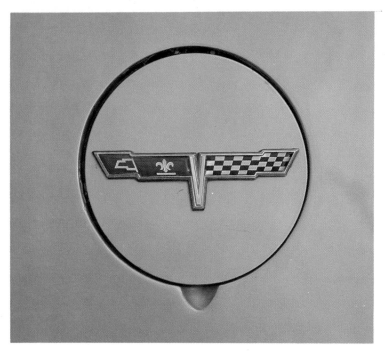

THE BIG BLOCK YEARS AND THE NEW SHAPE

The biggest changes for the '69 cars were under the skin, as quality control problems were sorted out. The 'Stingray' name returned, now condensed to one word.

Into the Seventies

'If all you want', said *Road and Track*, 'is blinding acceleration – buy one.'

Car & Driver agreed that this was 'the best Corvette ever'.

The prognosis was supported shortly afterward when the L88-powered versions took to the racetracks again – after Chevrolet had played the long-established homologation game with the FIA, and had not built anywhere near the minimum 500 required hardtops they said they had – and blew away everything in sight.

The near-rapture with which the l969 Corvette was greeted on all sides (except the Cobra owners' club) signaled the return of Zora Duntov as Chief Engineer of Corvette, and was proof positive that the Duntov magic was still as efficacious as ever, despite his short absence.

Chevrolet's quality-control problem had been caused by the speed at which the new model had been rushed on to the production lines in the last few months before its debut, and also by the logistical problems that arose when an auto maker of their size attempted to push a specialist sportscar into volume production. Even with the poor reputation that the 1968 models had acquired, sales had climbed once more, and 29,874 left St Louis during the calendar year.

For 1969, Duntov and his team had worked their way through the car from end to end, eliminating all the minor niggles and complaints that had been voiced by owners and magazine testers. The 1969 Corvette owned a whole list of revisions and alterations of a minor nature which, added together, transformed the car entirely and were the closest thing to an admission of guilt that any auto maker is ever likely to make. And, almost as if to mark the return of Duntov to the Corvette fold (or perhaps it was the other way round), the hallowed name which had been missing for that one in-between year was revived: condensed now to one word, the Stingray came back to the street.

With the ending of quality-control foul-ups, Chevrolet began to

speak of Corvette as a luxury sportscar. Unlike the Thunderbird, of which the phrase was more than passingly reminiscent, it did not grow any extra seats. But it was given the beginnings of a whole string of luxury extras, kicking off with inertia reel belts. Over the years this 'extra' game would proliferate to include tinted windows with shadeband, rear defogger, tilt/telescope steering, cruise control and so on; eventually *Car & Driver* would refer to the option list as Corvette's 'life-of-Reilly appurtenances'.

All pictures: It's hard to tell this 1969 from a '68, although the grilles are different, as are the hoods and standard wheels.

CORVETTE

INTO THE SEVENTIES

CORVETTE

For 1969, the new seatbelts were supplemented by a massive array of facia warning lights designed to alert the driver to any number of untoward happenings, like open doors or partly raised headlights. While it was still possible to specify a choice of drivetrain, selecting any one of four transmissions, six axle ratios and five engines, each car that left the plant carried a dash plaque stating which engine had been fitted. And since the rev limit on each engine was different, each tachometer was individually selected, with a marked redline appropriate to the situation. These little touches were indicative of the great care and attention being paid to each car as it made its trip along the assembly line, and signaled the high level of build quality perhaps more eloquently than any other single factor outside of the finished product itself.

This was a milestone year as well, for 1969 saw the introduction of Chevrolet's 350ci version of the smallblock V8. Over the years this

Changes for 1970 included revised fender vents and other detail changes to front parking lights. Otherwise unchanged, this would be the appearance of Corvette until 1973.

INTO THE SEVENTIES

CORVETTE

The 1970 Corvette *(top left)* differs hardly at all from the 1971 *(bottom left)*. The fender vent *(above left)* was now complex and chrome-plated. A rear luggage carrier was a frequently-fitted extra. Corvette now has no trunk worth speaking of and the carrier was therefore highly useful.

gradually replaced all the other engine options and survives today as the only engine offered in Corvette. In base trim it produced 300hp at 4800rpm; it was a sign of the times that its output closer to the tacho redline was not quoted, although it was acknowledged that 11:1 heads could give it another 50hp at 5800rpm.

There was also another engine option that year; the GM policy of non-involvement in motor racing now produced yet another winning combination as the aluminum powerplant originally destined for the Corvette Grand Sport resurfaced. Instead of using Duntov's l6-plug head the aluminum block was mated to the aluminum heads already available for the L88 engine; added together, they gave Corvette a top end in the region of 185mph. This combination was designated ZL1 and was part of the efforts made by the McLaren team in what was to be a highly successful assault on the Can Am series, which amounted to virtual domination.

Although the ZL1 had all the lightweight benefits of aluminum it was still strong at the bottom, and delivered all the power the racers could ask for, making it a fearsome tool. The big problem with the engine was that once it was tuned to the grenade limit – as race engines frequently are – the sensitivity of aluminum to heat expansion and contraction made it extremely prone to explosive detonation. It was a problem that raises its head all too often with aluminum engines – and iron engines with aluminum heads can be just as bad, sometimes worse, thanks to the different coefficients of iron and aluminum.

This was a problem from which the highly tuned L88 frequently suffered. In roadgoing trim, however, it remained the Corvette's street killer with the ZL1 the chief racetrack tool. But with all that, it was possible for any customer to order a Corvette with a ZL1 engine. They were built very slowly and carefully, in conditions of surgical precision and cleanliness; and in the now-established tradition, a mandatory part of the ZL1 specification was deletion of heater, air conditioning and power steering. As it came from the factory, the ZL1 Corvette weighed 2900lbs and could clock 12-second, 115mph quarter-mile times with ease; some small amounts of work on the

INTO THE SEVENTIES

1971 LT-1 Corvette Stingray.

CORVETTE

INTO THE SEVENTIES

CORVETTE

Left: 1972 models were as Corvette should be. Production was steady. Quality now much improved and popularity was soaring. The 350 smallblock V8 *(above)* would soon become standard for the make.

engine (like junking the cast-iron manifolds and allowing the engine to breathe) could change that to 11/115mph without too much difficulty.

After all the efforts at ironing out problems on the production line, the new super-smooth 1969 models were held up for two months by a strike. Because that would have delayed introduction of the new models anyway, and kept figures down, the decision to run the '69 model year on longer was taken by someone who was soon to have a profound effect on the nature of the Corvette, and indeed the automobile industry generally: John Z. DeLorean.

Because of this decision to run on, production figures for the 1969 car are somewhat distorted: calendar year sales showed a drop back to 24,791, with production during the same period running at 27,540. Production figures for the 1969 model year broke a record, although for the wrong reasons, and 38,762 of these excellent vehicles were built, a figure that would not be exceeded in a straight production year until 1973.

A survey sent to buyers of new Corvettes in January and February of 1969 revealed that they had a median age of 27 years and an income of around $14,500 (Corvette was listed at $4,402 base at the time); competitive make trade-in was well up over the previous year, as also were the number of first-time buyers. One way and another it was a pretty good set of results for Corvette – on one side of the paper. Over the page were the questions about the new Corvette these people had all bought. Thirty-seven percent were back at the dealers within an average of 3300 miles, complaining about panel fit, exterior finish, and body noises and gas mileage – which was understandably lower than other Chevrolet products. Worse still, 90 percent of new Corvettes needed more than normal service during the first two months.

This, however, was not the sort of information that was made public at the time. The kind of thing released to the press was the fact that Corvette number 250,000 had been built – and sold. The keys were handed over to the lucky buyer in a blaze of publicity. George

CORVETTE

Dyer, from Montebello, California, had paid $5000 (including extras) for his Riverside Gold Corvette, one of the 43 percent of coupes built that year, and traded a Barracuda to get it.

The only item that could be better than that was the other half of the publicity designed to highlight the reaching of the quarter-million mark, and that was the search by *Corvette News* for the oldest existing Corvette. An advert placed in this publication pulled over 70 replies from 24 different states – and all of them concerned one or more of the 300 Corvettes hand-built at Flint during the summer of 1953. Although there was sadly no trace of Job One, or even Number Two, the oldest existing Corvette was E53F001003, and it's the last digit that is significant. Numbering started at 1001, making this one the third ever built.

Located on a ranch in California, it turned out that its owner, Ed Thiebaud, was a collector, and had a total of eleven Corvettes stashed away in an old airplane hangar. Two more of those were built in l953 as well – Ed Thiebaud had numbers 3, 60 and 157. The 74 1953 models traced by Corvette News ran from 3 to 292, and the whole project stoked up more than a sufficiency of interest.

Meanwhile, John DeLorean was hard at work on the new Corvettes due out for 1970. The problems in '68 – which by the sound of that survey hadn't altogether been cleared up early in 1969 – were exactly the sort of thing that DeLorean was good at. Here was a man who knew what was needed. It was the same medicine that everybody in Detroit was being forced to swallow at the same time and was the

result of a number of extraneous factors, not least of which were the environmentalists et al. It was the waning of the musclecar era, the end of the three-page option list, it was good-bye to the sales brochures that spelled out performance in pure horsepower terms.

This was the year that saw GM make a commitment to low-compression engines suitable for unleaded gas in line with the 1970 Clean Air Act. Sealed carburetors and evaporative emission control followed, and suddenly the performance car was dead. Soon Pontiac was hard at work shedding the GTO image they had carefully built up and nurtured through the years. They weren't alone in this, as Chevrolet dumped the SS designation which had signified the performance versions of their passenger cars. Then in late 1970 Ford aban-

Left: Exhausts still make their exit through the bodywork. 1972 was the last year that there would be a Corvette with a chrome front.
Right: Chevrolet studio shot illustrates what was coming up for the 1973 model year.

1973, and the enthusiasts were unanimous in their dislike of Corvette's new plastic nosecone.

CORVETTE

INTO THE SEVENTIES

doned most of its Trans Am, USAC and NASCAR events, and began to tone down the Mustang to face the austerity to come, producing tame and weakened cars, allocating to the original Ponycar the same fate of emasculation suffered by its predecessor, the Thunderbird.

What DeLorean did could be summed up in one word: rationalization. Corvette had been pushed as America's only volume-built true sportscar for almost 20 years. In order to back that claim up it had been possible to order it with a huge variety of different performance packages – like the drag-race-only 4.56:1 back end, which was fitted to only 20 out of 1969's huge 38,000-unit run. Now these were all about to vanish slowly, as the option list was pruned and shifted away from performance, and DeLorean concentrated on building up the luxury image for Corvette.

The first changes in 1970 included small alterations to parking lights and grille, tinted glass as standard, and extra headroom, which was gained by changing the seats, not altering the roofline. This was just the beginning, however. To go with the dress-up program, DeLorean pushed for more and more production, a forced march which had already been proved detrimental to individual quality of the car. And he committed Corvette to a policy of planned rises in price, working on the basis that if you can sell all the cars you build the obvious next step is to build more and charge more for them: the 1970 Corvette had a base price which, at $5192, represented almost a whole $1000 increase over 1969. While the policy cannot have failed to delight the 14th floor of the GM HQ in Detroit, it was completely at odds with the original thinking behind the Corvette launch all those years before, and was clearly not one guaranteed to score points with Corvette purists.

Below and right: The 1973 cars set a standard which would last for 10 years with practically no alteration.
Above: Corvette Chief Engineer, Dave McLellan took over in January 1975 from Zora Duntov.

The fact that 1970 brought the introduction of Corvette's biggest engine ever, the massive 454, should not be taken as a sign that all was still well with those who saw Corvette as the ultimate expression of domestic power and performance. Rather it was the reverse. This

CORVETTE

INTO THE SEVENTIES

CORVETTE

Top left: Now with plastic front and rear, this was the 1975 Stingray.
Bottom left: It was also the convertible's farewell performance, as falling demand since the introduction of the t-top coupe had sealed its fate.
Above: New alloy wheels appeared in 1976, the last year that Corvette carried a Stingray nameplate.

huge big-block powerplant was – in LS5 form – less powerful, in street trim, than had been its smaller predecessor, the 427.

With one four-barrel carburetor, a 10.25:1 compression ratio and the beginnings of emission control add-ons, it produced a lowly 390hp. However, this again was quoted at 4800rpm, and the figure is likely to have been respectably healthier another 1000rpm further up the scale, a possibility backed up by its monstrous 500lbs/ft of torque, which was reached down at 3400rpm.

The LS6 was a different story: the aluminum heads that had done so much good work for Corvette in the past were called into action yet again, and helped this engine deliver a whopping 460hp, but it was only available for the one year. By 1971 it had been emasculated, and delivered 425hp, at the same time as the LS5 dropped back to 365hp. By 1972 the LS6 was gone completely and the LS5 was down to a miserable 270hp, although it was then that the way Detroit expressed its figures began to change, so the real difference in output wasn't as large as it sounded.

The vast multiplication of emission-control systems and the need to meet more and more stringent regulations in this area was at the root of all this. Positive Crankcase Ventilation had been introduced as far back as 1964, and Chevrolet had uprated to Air Injection by 1966; by 1975 all this would have escalated to full catalytic converter systems.

But this was only part of the story. There was also the coming end to lead additives in gasoline. Lead is added to gasoline as an anti-

knock ingredient, and its presence allows engines to run on a much higher compression ratio than would be possible without it. For example, the L88 engine really needed to use research or aviation gas at around 103 octanes in order to produce the desired result. Now it was made clear that in the future all that would be available would be an unleaded 91-octane fuel. Added to an L88 this could only spell expensive disaster, and therefore it was clear that Corvette – and every other car – would have to move toward low-power, low-compression engines. Chevrolet began moves to comply with the forthcoming regulations during 1970, and compression ratios were lowered as engine timing was altered.

This program killed off the successor to the Corvette's string of big-power engines, the LS7, since it too would have needed 103-octane aviation spirit to survive. That meant that the 425hp version of the LS6 was the only real performance option for the year, along with the 365hp big-block and two variants of the 350 smallblock, in either 270 or 330hp form.

The best news of the period was that the long overrun of 1969 models had made 1970 a very short production year, and only slightly more than 17,000 units were built. In the hands of DeLorean and Duntov this extra time and the slower production rate was not used to make all those tiny little changes to the car normally deemed necessary by Detroit each year. Instead it was put to good use, clearing up any lingering faults on the production line completely, and gradually St Louis went a long way to eradicating all the problems that had plagued the Corvette since its new body style of 1968.

A lengthy and rigorous new post-build quality-control procedure was instituted which involved a much longer testing sequence designed to pick up faults before the cars left the plant. As part of this program, and again as a result of fuel shortages and the general trend toward rationalization, the number of options available was slashed once more. By the time the 1972 models were announced there were

INTO THE SEVENTIES

All pictures: The 1976 cars have built-in alarms operated by the key just ahead of the 'Stingray' logo on the left fender. Since the plastic rear was introduced in 1974 the exhausts now clear the body from below.

CORVETTE

CORVETTE

two 350ci engines available, in 200 and 355hp form, and just one 454 big-block, now delivering its lowly 270hp, which was all it managed to drag from its 9:1 compression. There were still three transmissions to choose from: a three-speed automatic and a choice between a four-speed manual and the close-ratio Muncie box. There was still an assortment of axles to blend in – five different ratios were still available.

As the options decreased, however, so also did the personal care and attention that was given to each vehicle; the days when a Corvette fresh from the dealer could be a nice car to go to the golf club in or a no-holds barred drag racer were ended. By 1973 the sticker price for a base model had risen to $5400, and power steering, power windows, power brakes and a fairly basic FM radio were all extras which hiked the price even further. The three transmissions were still offered, there was one less final drive ratio, the compression ratio in the 454 was down to 8.25:1 and the two 350 options gave either 250 or 190hp. And this was the year of the serious fuel shortages, when Britain brought home its own oil from the North Sea and the Arab countries entered the game of international power politics with an embargo on oil sales. As Americans began to shoot each other at the pumps in the quest for gas, the future of the sportscar had never seemed quite so bleak. Yet the 1973 Corvette brought a major face-lift for the first time since 1968 – the original Sting Ray had been completely revised in less time – and had quite simply never looked better.

Along with the changes in Federal regulations concerning horse-power advertising, lead-free gas and emission-control equipment, there were other requirements concerned with highway safety. They

concerned things like bumper height and impact resistance, plus side-impact protection, and compliance with these began to cost Corvette a little weight.

In order to meet side-impact requirements the fiberglass doors had to be reinforced with steelwork: a move that in a way robbed the car of all the advantages of fiberglass construction, with the exception of the anti-corrosion benefits. In addition the front had to be able to withstand the Federal 5mph crash test. The sharply pointed Corvette snout, with what amounted to a token piece of chromework signifying

All pictures: By 1977, with the body shape basically 9 years old and the chassis older, Corvette was widely tipped for a facelift, but it was not to be.

1978 was the Corvette's Silver Anniversary year. Along with a rather more discreet package came this Indy Pace Car replica.

CORVETTE

CORVETTE

Simplicity returns in 1979. The elegant glassback had been available in the aftermarket for some time. Liftback conversions were also on sale – but not from Chevrolet.

a bumper, was not strong enough. Stronger bumpers out front would have worked, but would have damaged the clean styling lines considerably.

GM had been using plastic fronts on various cars for a while; face-on shots of the last GTO would have shown a polyurethane nosepiece, and it was to this material that Corvette engineers now turned. They placed a fender strong enough to take the 5mph impact and more besides inside it, fixed directly to the chassis rails with impact-absorbing bolts. The nosecone was filled with a lightweight honeycomb material which by itself surpassed the 5mph requirements. The basic shape remained unchanged, but Corvette now had its own body color wraparound nosecone.

The whole item added about two inches to the car's overall length, and the package for 1973 put Corvette up from just over 3300lbs to just over 3700lbs. All of the extra length, and most of the weight was up front. The vents that had decorated the rear of the front fenders were tidied up, and the change in its appearance seems to have been along the same lines as the general trend toward economy and cleanliness that had affected the original Sting Ray during its lifetime. But this time there was little applause from Corvette fans, most of whom seemed to regard the new plastic front end as a step backward rather than forward although to modern eyes, now used to this type of front-end treatment, it is elegant in its own right, and to many a positive improvement.

More improvements were afoot in Detroit as the NVH (Noise, Vibration and Harshness) squads had been round again, and had eliminated more rattles and road noise, largely by adding some extra soundproofing, and this too contributed to the extra weight. When Corvette had been a powerhouse racer owners were reasonably prepared to live with some of its imperfections, to allow it some drawbacks – like interior noise – and saw them as part of the price of having all that brute power on tap. But now there was no brute power available, nobody wanted a slow car that was unpleasant to drive. Most of the sound-deadening mats went under the hood and inside the passenger footwells, and blocked out engine roar and road noise.

Having said all that, the Corvette was still by no means slow, especially by modern standards. Any car that could deliver standing

CORVETTE

quarters in 14 seconds/90mph had to be doing something right, and a top speed over 130mph was nothing to complain about either. That kind of performance was only available from the 454, of course; the two 350 engines couldn't approach those kind of figures.

Another major change also arrived in 1973: steel-belted radial tires. The superiority of this type of tire needs no real explanation now. Fitting it to Corvette (and a number of other Chevrolet models) went a long way to improving handling, especially Corvette's well-known trick of throwing the back end away on a wet road. Thay gave a longer life as well, and also met Duntov's personal requirement that they should be safe at the maximum speed the stock Corvette was capable of – standard practice now, when tire technology has advanced so much in the last decade, but by no means commonplace in the early seventies.

Their arrival also saw the end of some of the ride harshness that had been a feature of the car from the very beginning. Duntov asked his engineers to address themselves to the problem now because radials have different characteristics, and pass different vibrations up from the road than other tires. Rubber mounts were fitted between body and frame, and this removed most of the vibration, making the '73 models a quieter and more civilized drive.

To go with the radials new aluminum wheels were introduced, the now-familiar dished and slotted design which was not replaced until 1984. The same width as the steel wheels, they were slightly lighter, reducing unsprung weight.

Despite the fact that the purists were apparently offended by the

All pictures: By 1979 the need for a new Corvette was becoming more and more obvious. Minor changes to spoilers and airdams made an elegant shape look heavy and clumsy, but rumors of a mid-engined car were not fulfilled.

new-look Corvette, sales in 1973 began to climb again. They had dipped down after the near-30,000 high in 1968, bottomed at 22,000 in 1970 and were beginning a gradual rise, making it through 26,652 in 1972, up again to 29,661 in 1973: and those are all calendar year sales figures – 1973 model year production went over 30,000, the first time it had happened genuinely, without the aid of an extended production period.

Corvette watchers reasoned that the increases in sales were in part due to the fact that Corvette was now attracting an entirely new type of buyer, one interested in looks and luxury rather than performance. Although the performance buyers were still there, the Corvette now had that indefinable something that is called style.

INTO THE SEVENTIES

CORVETTE

Style was increased in l974 by the addition of a new polyurethane back end. In body color, it too concealed the equipment necessary to meet the Federal 5mph impact tests but, incredibly, it encountered no opposition from Corvette fans, and was widely welcomed as a definite styling improvement. It matched the styling lines of the front exactly, and between them the two plastic moldings gave the Corvette a complete, overall 'look' which was most decidedly acceptable.

With minor variations, this was the design that would carry the Corvette for the next ten years, the longest that any body style has lasted. If we accept the new plastic cones as being 'minor' changes, the body shape introduced in 1968 lasted until the end of 1983, a staggering 15 years. Even more staggering is the fact that the Corvette in 1983 looked every bit as sleek, aggressive and downright attractive as it had done in 1968, possibly even more so.

Tiny changes marked the introduction of the 1975 models, although this was the first year that no convertibles were available. The percentage of buyers specifying the hardtop coupe – even though the clip-out backlight had been discontinued two years previously – had risen to almost 90 percent, so the convertible was rationalized into oblivion. Also departing, after ten years' sterling service, was the last variant of the big-block engine, and powerplant options for 1975 were either the 165hp L48 350 or the top-of-the-range L82 version, which could summon up 205hp. The 454 finally left the fold after failing the long-term emissions tests now required by the Federal government. Although it was 'clean' from new, it couldn't pass the 50,000-mile requirements and was dropped from Corvette, although it was still available in pickups and for a long time remained the most powerful engine available in any American 'car'. There were still three transmission options for Corvette though, and one of the four final drive ratios was the 'economy' 2.73:1.

Also missing from the Corvette line-up from January 1975 was another long-serving member of the family: this was the year in which Zora Duntov finally retired. His replacement as Corvette chief engineer was Dave McLellan, who had started working for GM in the Milford NVH labs in 1959, moving into the Chevrolet Engineering Center in 1971.

With 1974 a good year for sales, 1975 was expected to show a rise into the 30,000-plus bracket for the first time. In the middle of one of the most severe recessions to strike the auto industry that would have been good going. What happened was even better, as Corvette sales took an even steeper upturn and rocketed through the roof to 40,607. As prices climbed over $6000 for the base cars, with power brakes,

By 1980 Corvette development appeared to be at a standstill. Although behind-the-scenes work was proceeding, the car was essentially 12 years old outside, older under the skin.

INTO THE SEVENTIES

A full-house Eckler conversion on a 1980 Corvette. The cost of the body panels could double its price, if not its value.

CORVETTE

power steering and factory air still extras, Corvette was a runaway success. Most of the year's production was committed by about April, and there were long waiting lists all over the country.

With that kind of popularity going for it, changes for 1976 were again slight, since GM reasoning was still running the same way: why change when you're so far ahead of the game? Once more the answer in this situation is always the same: build more and put the price up again. Which doesn't mean that no one at Chevrolet had any intentions of moving ahead – there were plenty of good ideas around. Even top management cannot have ignored the fact that one of the prime functions of a flagship like Corvette is to stay out in front, and that sooner or later things would have to be different. Apart from anything else the frame beneath Corvette's sexy new body had been

designed in 1968. Good as it was, it would have to be replaced in the not-too-distant future.

But what Chevrolet had on their hands meantime was not only the most popular Corvette ever, but the most popular sportscar ever. It remained unchanged, apart from a few positive items like the switch to catalytic converters and breakerless electronic ignition and a new dash design, until the end of 1977. It was in that year, at 2.01 pm on the afternoon of March l5, to be exact, that Chevrolet general manager Robert D.Lund drove the 500,000th Corvette off the line in a year when sales again hit a new high, up from 41,673 in 1976 to an enormous 49,213.

However, 1978 was an even more momentous year for Corvette, since it was 25 years old. The biggest change to the body was the

CORVETTE

switch away from the sugar-scoop rear aspect and the arrival of a wraparound glassback, which made Corvette even better looking than before. The glassback wasn't a major engineering change and involved little in the way of retooling. The biggest criticism of it was that although it increased the luggage load area, it wasn't a liftback tailgate, which would seem to be an obvious choice. Indeed, there were a number of aftermarket conversion kits available almost as soon as the car was first shown.

In fact the decision on the glassback had been made as far back as 1974, and a liftback had been considered. Proposals for both fixed and opening backlight had been sent to GM management: the opening tailgate tooled up for $4 million, the fixed one for $2 million. Although the fixed unit went into production for 1978 it had been changed, by 1980, to a liftback in response to demand.

Demand was also high for the specially badged Silver Anniversary models, which featured special paintwork and every extra known to the GM order blank. Base price for the Corvette was $9000 in 1978; the Silver Anniversary came out with a sticker price of $12,500, but it would have been a very strange car salesman who let one out of the showroom without a premium, and the bidding usually began at around $500 over sticker.

This was also the year of the Indy Pace Car, and as people began to expect more and more that the arrival of the new-shape Corvette would be announced at any moment Chevrolet began a whole series of 'limited edition' tricks to cover up the fact that although the new Corvette was coming once again, it would be slightly delayed.

By 1982 the Mitchell/Shinoda body had reached its final appearance. The front air dam looked clumsy, but actually worked, aiding both stability and gas mileage as it cleaned up airflow around Corvette's massive frontal aspect.

By 1982 Corvette came from the factory with the liftback which had first been a non-standard conversion. And the weight-saving glassfiber single leaf rear spring was a feature of this model too.

INTO THE SEVENTIES

XP-700 first appeared in 1958, but was reworked to give this appearance in 1960.

The Show Cars and the Experimentals

Continual revision of existing ideas in engineering and styling is a constantly necessary part of an auto maker's survival kit. While styling details are largely a matter of taste and can be test-marketed in advance, engineering innovation needs to be thoroughly tested in a working environment before it can be given a production application. For many car builders that fact, combined with the obvious publicity benefits, is a justification for a race program at one or several levels.

In the fifties there were a number of European sportscar makers who maintained a high racetrack visibility for their cars by running experimentals or prototypes in competition. While this brought immediate publicity rewards it also attracted criticisms along the general lines that the vehicle on the racetrack bore little or no relation to the product in the dealers' windows. The answer to that, of course, was that although it might not do so at the time it would do sooner or later.

When Duntov joined Corvette as an ex-race driver it would seem to have been natural for him to take Corvette onto the circuits to conduct his development work, but although he could see the benefits – and addressed the SAE on exactly that topic in 1953 – he was not keen to do so. In fact he told Karl Ludvigsen, 'I was pushed into it'.

The tricked-up Corvette that went to Sebring was a track version of a road car. Against the race specials of Jaguar, Ferrari, Mercedes and Porsche it was out of its depth. A race car would have had to be built, and would have had to be developed separately from but alongside the production Corvette. It was this two-pronged approach to Corvette development that Cole was anxious to promote, but as Chevrolet General manager he had plenty of other important things to occupy his attention.

In 1956 Harley Earl borrowed an engineless Jaguar D-type; he planned to alter its appearance to disguise its provenance, add a Chevrolet V8 and take it racing, Duntov was opposed to this and argued strongly in favor of a purpose-built Chevrolet race car which would be to Corvette what the D-type was to the XK series. Almost in confirmation of that, the body that was placed on to a 92in frame (the stock Corvette was 102in) at Chevrolet styling was extremely reminiscent of the D-type's flowing curves: in fact, it looked more like a Jaguar than a Corvette.

The body shape was given warm approval in the upper echelons of Chevrolet and GM. The car was designated XP 64 and construction of four units was authorized. Duntov was assigned a staff and given the go-ahead in October 1956. The work was done in a corner of the Chevrolet Engineering Center over a period of months leading up to the official release date on March 21, 1957, when the Corvette SS, as it had become officially known, was described as both 'startling' and 'experimental' by Ed Cole.

Certainly the construction methods had been both of those things. The design team concentrated all their efforts on the car in that small corner of the workshop, and while the engineers labored over their boards the craftsmen translated drawings into metal, so that it was possible to view plans and reality at the same time.

The frame was nothing like the stock Corvette's. It was a lightweight spaceframe of some complexity which demonstrated great torsional strength yet weighed only 180lbs. Its rigidity allowed the use of lightweight magnesium for the bodyshell.

Other weight-saving techniques were employed, and these included the use of fiberglass to construct an irregularly shaped 43-gallon fuel tank. When it was finished, the Corvette SS weighed 1850lbs dry against the production Corvette's 2800lbs.

The engine was the 283 V8, but it used aluminum heads and an alloy oil pan to give it an all-in weight of about 450lbs, saving about 80lbs over the stock engine. With fuel injection and some port work by Duntov it developed over 300hp at 6400rpm.

Top: The interior of Mako Shark 11 was clean and tidy as well as futuristic and operational – no mean achievement.
Below: The 200mph CERV 1 single-seater.

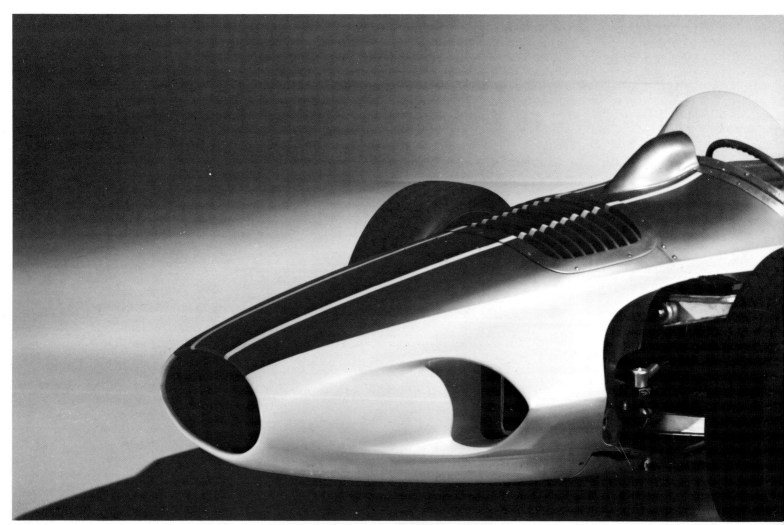

CORVETTE

THE SHOW CARS AND THE EXPERIMENTALS

CORVETTE

Left: Corvette SS gets concentrated workshop attention.
Above: Standing round the spaceframe chassis, Duntov (with cigarette) discusses details with stylists Clare MacKichan (standing to Duntov's right, arms folded) and Ed Donaldson (on MacKichan's right).

At the car's unveiling Ed Cole said that it was strictly a research project to study, 'advanced engineering characteristics in the field of performance, handling, braking and other safety features'. He also said . . .

'it is the engineering department's job in this area of design to create and test various components such as engine, brakes and drive-train, and explore new suspension principles.

Testing under the most severe operating conditions gives engineers the chance to study the performance and safety characteristics of new developments and features which have been built into this vehicle.

That is the principle behind the development of the Corvette SS. It is a study of new ideas to determine whether they might eventually be refined and offered in regular passenger cars.

Testing over tough race courses will serve to quickly furnish comparative engineering data that, under ordinary circumstances, would require long periods of research.'

Testing was conducted prior to competition at the 1957 Sebring event, using a pre-production prototype chassis. Test drives were handled first by Duntov and then by Juan Manuel Fangio and Stirling Moss. Fangio broke his own own record at Sebring during the test session, Moss was fractionally slower. In fact, the session was so successful that Fangio was contracted to drive for Chevrolet at Sebring provided a car could be guaranteed – it couldn't, and Fangio appeared for Maserati. Moss was approached, but was already committed. Chevrolet signed a Texan race driver, Carroll Shelby, but he too grew impatient as the event drew nearer and there were no race-ready cars. In the end Shelby too raced for Maserati and the SS was handled by John Fitch and Piero Taruffi.

It proved to be one of the fastest sportscars in the world, and only the 4.5-liter Maseratis could pull away from it. A handling problem caused by collapsed bushing in the chassis led to its retirement, but the trouble was minor and it was clear that the SS could be exceptionally competitive. But before it could make its planned outing at Le Mans the AMA adopted their no-race resolution, and the project was simply and abruptly halted.

The chassis which had been used as a mobile testbed at Sebring had been returned to Chevrolet, stripped down and cleaned up, but never finished. With the cancellation of the project the SS body it should have worn was simply never built, and it remained in the workshop with no apparent purpose in life and no foreseeable future.

Officially, that is.

When Harley Earl retired in 1958 his successor was William L. 'Bill' Mitchell. Almost his first act was to obtain that testbed chassis; he wanted it for a project of his own and it was ideally suited to the purpose. Despite the AMA resolution and the wholehearted GM adoption of it as policy, Mitchell planned to go racing.

In order to do so without contravening the new rules he had to give his race car a name and an appearance that were not identifiably from the Chevrolet stable. As head of styling the change of image was the least of his problems, and with Larry Shinoda he created a low, flat body still with a hint of the original Corvette SS and traces of the D-type Jaguar which had inspired it, but it was in fact far more modern in overall style. The body was built by early 1959 and the engine, since development in this area had been halted, was almost identical to the Corvette SS, although its rated output was rather lower, at 280hp.

Although Mitchell was head of styling and a GM Vice-President, his activities did not represent a covert skirting of the AMA ban by the company. He financed the car from his own resources and even then only just persuaded GM to allow him to become involved in racing at all. And Zora Duntov was, again, opposed to the race involvement. Having been dragged into it with the original SS against his will, he now felt that without corporate support the new car would never do as well as it should have done, and might actually produce adverse publicity.

Named the Sting Ray, it made its debut appearance in an SCCA event at Marlboro in April of 1959 with Dr Richard Thompson at the wheel. Despite Duntov's misgivings, the Sting Ray made an immediate impression on all who saw it. The most frequently heard description was 'futuristic'. And if its appearance was impressive so too was its performance. Thompson's efforts in that first race verged on the superhuman, despite an almost diabolical handling problem which was largely the legacy of a braking system that had only two positions: on or off. Unfortunately they were generally on when they should have been off and off when they should have been on. Thompson drove round these difficulties for much of the race but eventually they got the better of him and the car spun out. By the time it was back on the tarmac and restarted the best Thompson could manage was a not-too-disappointing fourth.

In most ways, however, it had been a suitably impressive first race, although the SCCA were somewhat unimpressed with Thompson's own performance. The brutal nature of the handling combined with his grim determination to win had led him into a rather cavalier display which earned him a 90-day suspension from SCCA events.

While this penalty ran its course the car made a number of USAC appearances during which serious attempts were made to cure the braking problem, but by the time the car came back to SCCA it still hadn't been solved, and the Sting Ray still demonstrated a vicious tendency to swap ends.

In part this was caused by the new-shape body Mitchell and Shinoda had created. Its aerodynamic qualities were better than the current production Corvettes, and allowed it to travel faster. Although the massive 11in drum brakes were good enough on the road cars they simply weren't beefy enough to cope with the higher speeds of which the Sting Ray was capable. The situation was further complicated by the tendency of the body to lift at speed. The flat wedge shape should have kept the car pressed downward, but the reverse was happening. Shimming the rear axle to lower the nose and increase the angle of attack went some way toward alleviating this, but still didn't help with the braking faults.

The situation remained the same throughout 1959, but in 1960 the Sting Ray reappeared with a newly built and much lighter body, plus sintered brake linings and a single power booster rather than the

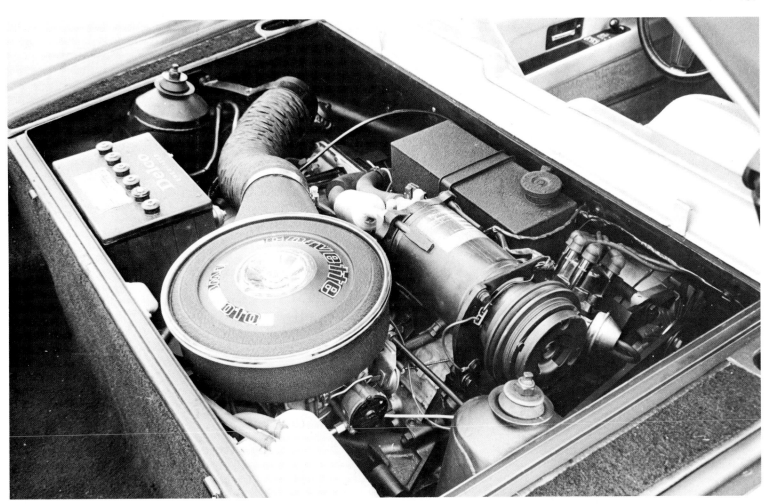

Below left: The XP 987 GT proved that Corvette's appearance could have changed radically if finance allowed.
Above: Mid-mounted rotary engine couldn't meet emission regulations.
Below: Wind-tunnel testing of models played a vital role in shaping bodywork.

complex double-pumper it had used before. That the problem could have been cured by the installation of disk brakes was well appreciated, but the lack of money for research and tooling ruled this option out completely.

However, the winter's work had made it seem like a different car, and throughout the 1960 season Thompson became involved in a series of epic battles which eventually left him clear winner of the SCCA C Modified Championship for the year.

The following year, cleaned and painted, with windshields and other comforts, and bearing badges that read 'Corvette', the Sting Ray became what Chevrolet described as an 'experimental' car of 'ultra-modern jet-stream design'. Its appearance as a show car was credited to 'a last-minute decision by Ed Cole'.

The fact was that the planned replacement for the Corvette was due out in 1962 but had run into a number of hitches which had caused its demise, and in 1963 Mitchell's Sting Ray was to fill the bill left by the cancellation of the mid-engined project.

After the termination of the ill-fated Q-car, Duntov, with Ed Cole's knowledge and backing, had been looking at ways to get some form of mid-engined vehicle into production. The Q-car had been canceled largely because of the immense tooling costs involved in placing a transaxle to carry transmission and differential in one unit at the back, changing the weight balance and thus the handling. Duntov's argument now was that thinking should be taken a little further down the line and that a full mid-engine layout was the next obvious step.

The same problems of economics still beset the project, however, and in 1959 the decision to go ahead and design Corvette's new persona around Mitchell's Sting Ray was taken. But Duntov continued with his examination of and experimentation with mid-engined layout, this time using as a basis the Chevrolet Experimental Racing Vehicle (CERV 1).

It was envisaged that this car would have to compete in a suitably high-visibility event in order to achieve its purpose and was thus designed around the dimensional requirements for Indianapolis, although the primary objective was to be a further assault on the Pike's Peak hill climb.

Although the mid-engine layout adopted for it gave handling advantages straight away, Duntov employed more weight-saving techniques than ever before. The 283 smallblock engine was constructed entirely from aluminum this time, using a new casting process that allowed it to run without liners. Great use of other alloys, particularly magnesium, was made in the castings for things like the water pump, clutch housing, inlet manifold and starter motor.

The engine used mostly stock parts inside: pistons, crank, bear-

CORVETTE

Left: *above and below* XP-700 was more than just a show car.
Above: The sleek Corvette 4-rotor featured a long, sloping tail.
Right: The sketches based on a Jaguar D-type which were the starting-point for the Corvette SS.

ings and Duntov cam were all standard items, but it weighed 150lbs less than the stock smallblock motor and delivered 353hp from its 283ci swept volume.

The chassis for CERV was a lightweight (125lbs) spaceframe unit in chrome steel, mounting Corvette SS independent front suspension and a new independent setup for the rear. The rear brakes were cast aluminum finned drums and were mounted inboard, directly to the alloy-cased differential. The drive shafts then were fixed by universal joints at each end and formed the upper links in the parallelogram arrangement. This arrangement was very similar to the one that had been in the pipeline for the Q-car, and thus was similar to the independent setup that would be making its appearance on the Corvette for 1963 onward – although for CERV Duntov used the more traditional coil-over-shock-absorber layout rather than the transverse leaf which Corvette was given.

First testing with CERV 1 at Pike's Peak was run in conjunction with Firestone, but showed some disappointing times. Firestone pulled out and the team left the Peak, only to discover afterward that their times were in some cases better than the record. More – private – testing was done in conjunction with Firestone and it was after two weeks at Riverside in November that CERV 1, now the Chevrolet Engineering Research Vehicle, was shown to an enthusiastic public as a prelude to the Grand Prix.

Engine capacity ruled it out of GP racing, but CERV was well suited to Indy, where the current speed record was marginally less than 180mph. In order to attain that many different options were examined, including the use of both a Roots-type supercharger and twin turbochargers. In this latter guise the small V8 engine was measured at close to 500hp, could lift the front wheels of CERV clear off the ground and could provoke wheelspin in third gear at over 100mph. But even that paled beside the performance of a bored-out 377 with fuel injection, which averaged 206mph around the GM proving ground at Milford in 1964.

The next obvious step for CERV was the construction of CERV 2. Duntov envisaged this as a two-seat sportscar, much closer to Corvette than any single-seater could be – and also far closer to the parallel development of race machine and roadgoing sportscar which Cole had wanted, and had fallen by the wayside with the death of the SS project in 1957.

The CERV 2 project was given the go-ahead by Bunkie Knudsen,

but even as the work was begun on its construction GM leadership reaffirmed their support for the AMA resolution, and the rug was pulled from under the project.

Meanwhile there had been other developments on the show car circuit. Almost as a preparation for the forthcoming new Corvette Sting Ray, in April 1962 Chevrolet showed an experimental called the Mako Shark. This was an extension of the Sting Ray design which Mitchell had used for his race car, and Chevrolet had now 'adopted' almost formally.

Treatment for the Shark included a much-lengthened hood, which was now 81in long, with 44 of those overhanging the front. Preserving the lines of the Sting Ray racer meant keeping the sharp, almost beaked front edge, which in turn dictated invisible headlights. Rotating out from behind the grille as they would on the production car a year later, they were operated by small electric motors.

As a continuation of work being done with CERV 1, the Shark featured a 4-53 Roots blower built by GM's Detroit Diesel Division, although this was as close as it would ever come to production. Within months, however, the 1963 Sting Ray would be in production, and as soon as it was Mitchell started work on the Shark's successor: Mako Shark II.

The Shark II was destined to be to Corvette in the late sixties what Mitchell's Sting Ray had been at the beginning of the decade. Once again it was his own pet project conducted in close harmony with Larry Shinoda, and once again it was to be a completely practical and drivable show car. The commitment in this area was underlined when Mitchell insisted that it should be built on to an existing Corvette Sting Ray frame. From the outset he envisaged that its debut appearance would be as the center-stage star of the 1965 New York International Auto Show.

Mako Shark 11 in a typical GM Publicity shot.

CORVETTE

THE SHOW CARS AND THE EXPERIMENTALS

CORVETTE

All pictures: As it appeared in 1965, when the Sting Ray was only two years into production, Shark 11 already demonstrated the looks and features of the forthcoming 1968 Corvette, and some features which didn't make production for almost ten years.

Mitchell outlined the appearance he was looking for and left it to Shinoda and his team to translate the words and sketches into a full-size car. Like the Sting Ray before it this design was destined to be the basis of the restyle that would mark the arrival of the next Corvette generation in 1968. It was also destined to be one of the most eye-catching and singular styling exercises on the two-seat sportscar ever. Its lean and sleek elegance was matched only by its purposeful and hungry stance. It looked a million dollars and had the appearance of a car traveling at 200mph even when it was parked, although the big-block V8 with which is was equipped could have propelled it quite close to that.

When it made its appearance Chevrolet described it as Mako Shark II – The Experimental Corvette, and made sure that the word 'experimental' appeared several times in all of their news releases. But it would have been hard for anybody who saw it or read about it to form any other opinion, since Shark II was loaded to the roofline with experimental tricks and toys. Many of these would eventually surface on the production line of Corvette and other GM passenger cars, but not for a number of years. The remainder of them stayed 'experimental'.

The wipers, for example, retracted beneath a vacuum-operated cowl when not in use, a trick that was more stylish than functional (but it appeared in production for a short while). The steering wheel contained extra controls to tilt and telescope it for reach and angle, something that is reasonably commonplace now. But there was another control on the wheel which allowed the steering ratio to be altered by the driver but this has not become a production option.

The dashboard was reorganized to put the essential controls ahead of the driver and auxiliary instruments in a center console, an arrangement that was a feature of the revamped 1968 Corvette – although instrumentation in that car was traditional analog rather than the digital display which was a part of Shark II and has been a feature of Corvette from 1984 onward.

Also due to go into production shortly – and for a short while – was the fiber-optic monitoring system which informed the driver of any failure in the running lights. There were six headlights, which could be selected in a mixture of combinations according to visibility, and 'cornering lights' which shone through gills ahead of the front wheels when the turn signal was operated. Turn signals themselves were sequential at the rear.

Also a feature of the 1984 cars, and present on Shark II, is the clamshell hood, which swings forward to give unrivaled engine access. Shark also had two separate circular openings in the hood which allowed fluid levels to be checked and replenished without the need to open the hood fully. It had an adjustable rear spoiler as well, which was power-operated from the dashboard. This concept is one that followers of modern motor racing will be more than familiar with. In 1965 it was widely regarded as nothing more than a gimmick – except perhaps by those who were aware of the extent of Chevrolet involvement with Chaparral and the recent patents on adjustable spoilers.

When it was finished the Shark made a worldwide debut, which took it from Detroit to the prestigious Paris salon, then to London, Turin, Brussels and Geneva, receiving praise and accolades from the world's press everywhere it went. When it finally returned Bill Mitchell used it on the road from time to time, and it made frequent appearances as a pace car at assorted race venues.

After two years the Mako Shark II was more or less transformed into the 1968 Corvette facelift, although most of its more outrageous features were missing, especially those connected with the massive electronics package that had been installed behind the seats. But it was now less of a show car than living proof that designers' dreams can become reality, and so it was transformed from Shark II into the

THE SHOW CARS AND THE EXPERIMENTALS

Manta Ray, with a rearranged tail incorporating the sugar-scoop backlight now a feature of production Corvettes. Seen from the side this lengthened tail brought the rear fender lines to a pronounced point, but also effectively raised the roofline and carried it down toward the tail, giving it a slightly humpbacked look very similar to the clumsiness of the abandoned Corvette four-seater and the production XKE 2+2. It also lost its retractable rear bumper getting instead a body-color plastic arrangement in a material called Endura; this would surface on Corvette fronts in 1973 and tails in 1974.

Under the hood went the new, all-aluminum ZL-1 and Mitchell's favored side exhaust system appeared beneath the door edges. All things taken together, Shark had become Manta Ray, which had given it a new-enough face for its life as a show car to be extended briefly. But it was now too much like the production Corvette, and showgoers wanted to see the next step along the way rather than the last.

Duntov still believed firmly that the mid-engined layout was the only truly valid answer; while Mitchell and his stylists could adopt the latest pieces of automotive trickery and make a stunning show car capable of going into production, they did not represent any genuine engineering solutions or advances at all. Aside from its body, the Corvette on sale during 1983 was remarkably similar to the Corvette Sting Ray of 1963. Duntov was anxious to take Corvette engineering as far ahead as he could, and keep it at the front.

What held him back time after time was the cash investment required. As he worked studiously away at his various mid-engined projects the GM hierarchy continually changed position on the subject, leaving him in a constant stop – go situation. It was finally Dick Gerstenberg who stopped the mid-engined projects in 1972, once again on the basis that while Corvette was selling faster than it could be built there was absolutely no point in changing anything about it except the price. At the time the mid-engined car was as close as it had ever been to actual production, and this pretty Corvette could have been on the road by 1974-75.

The XP 880, which later became the Astro II show car, had come close, laid out as a simple mid-engined model Chevrolet could put into production quickly should Ford ever get their economy-version

Above and right: The Astro 111 show car belongs firmly in the ranks of experimental-only models.
Below: The mid-engined XP 880 – called Astro 11 – was shown in 1968 and could have made production.

GT40 into action. This scaled-down version of the famous racer had been around in 1967 and it was well known that Ford were keen to see it selling aganst Corvette. Astro II was a neat styling job on straightforward backbone chassis, and could have been a lot better than it was had there been a suitable transaxle to cope with the output from its mid-mounted V8. But there wasn't, and interest in creating one had died with the Q-car.

Building CERV II in response to Ford's endurance-racing ambitions, Duntov had created a mid-engined open two-seater which had overcome the problem another way. It had been four-wheel drive, and had used two separate torque converters, one at each end. Using the 377ci all-aluminum engine and swapping final drive ratios around gave CERV II a wide range of potential. It could do 0-60 in less

CORVETTE

THE SHOW CARS AND THE EXPERIMENTALS

CORVETTE

All pictures: The elegant 4-rotor photographed just before it left for the Paris Salon. The clean dash layout *(above)* featured an advanced digital readout in a special pod *(above left)*.

than 3 seconds, with a top speed around 115mph, or it could go 0-60 in 4 seconds and have a top speed in excess of 180mph.

This technique was used again on the XP 882, which Duntov saw as the logical development of the four-wheel drive 200mph CERV II into a roadgoing mid-engined Corvette. Unfortunately, the car was virtually stillborn, once again on purely economic terms. The argument against it said that it was no bigger, better or faster than Corvette, but it would cost more and therefore couldn't be sold. Ruling on this was one of the first decisions John DeLorean had to make when he took over at Chevrolet. He countered by proposing the K-car, a cheaper Corvette based around Camaro and supposedly costing $3500, but he met opposition to that suggestion from Duntov onward, and gave the idea up when he found that tooling up would make it just as costly as the existing Corvette.

XP 882 was resurrected briefly at the New York Show in 1970, principally as a counter to Ford's deal with De Tomaso which would put the Pantera in the Dearborn stable. It was received with such wild enthusiasm on all sides that DeLorean became an advocate of the mid-engine layout and gave his backing to further development work as well as altering the appearance. XP 882 had a fairly heavy front end, although in side view it looked very similar to the '82 Camaro/ Trans Am. After its facelift it was renamed (or renumbered) XP 895 and had a distinctly Italian flavor to it. It was also fairly overweight, and it was now that DeLorean began investigating the possibility of building an aluminum-bodied car for the first, but not last, time.

In fact an aluminum version was built. It worked well and tipped the scales at several hundred pounds less than a fiberglass body, but cost too much money. Only after spending many months, and even taking bids from all over Europe, did DeLorean abandon his plans for an aluminum-bodied Corvette, and the project was shelved.

Then in 1970 Chevrolet signed their deal with the holders of the Wankel patents, and began a brief but fast-paced flirtation with the rotary engine. DeLorean eventually became quite keen on the project. There were two rotary-powered Corvettes built, a two-rotor and a four-rotor, both with a mid-mounted layout. The 266ci two-rotor car was developed and constructed in a very short space of time and was

CORVETTE

Above and below: The GTP Corvette features joint efforts from a number of different companies, but carries the Corvette nameplate. Experiments with turbo power might have put the 1980 Turbo 11 Corvette *(left)* into production.

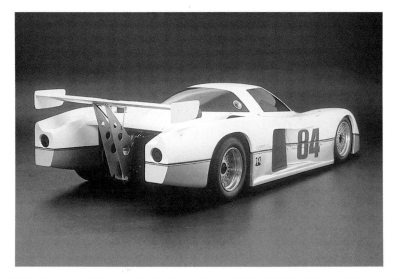

built in Italy by Pininfarina. Even with a body in sheet steel it weighed in at only 2600lbs. It was unveiled at Frankfurt early in September 1973, and by the time it had reached Paris for the October 4 opening of the Salon it had been joined by another, four-rotor Corvette.

Apart from its bigger, 390ci, engine, this was different in a number of other ways. It was built in Detroit by Duntov and his staff, and its higher displacement was purely down to the fact that it had been fitted with two two-rotor powerplants. Although the two-rotor was an elegant and civilized car, with performance roughly on a par with the base Corvette, the four-rotor was more equivalent to the big-block, and gave similar performance.

From conception to running automobile had taken only a few months. In large part that was because a body didn't have to be built: one existed. The four-rotor had been slipped into XP 882 in place of its mid-mounted V8; after the modified show car had proved its worth a new body was created for it and it was this exceptionally good-looking gullwing that followed the two-rotor to Paris.

It stopped there, and so did GM flirtation with the Wankel engine. GM had already said to Chevrolet that there would only be a new Corvette if it used a rotary powerplant. It was now clear that, for some time at least, there would be no new Corvette, and Mitchell's body design carried the flag for another whole decade.

The long-awaited Corvette restyle for the 1984 model year.

The Eighties and Beyond

Working on the shaping and styling of the body for the four-rotor car which went on to join the two-rotor on its world tour was Jerry Palmer, the man who would get the task of creating the restyled body for Corvette in the eighties. Under Palmer's guidance the look of Corvette from the late seventies and almost certainly into the nineteen nineties would be established. The engineering would be handled by Dave McLellan.

Certainly by the late seventies, as Corvette's 25th anniversary approached and the current model neared its own 15th birthday, it became clear that the arrival of the next Corvette generation was urgent. The Europeans and Japanese had established a clear ability to produce the right car: the cult of Datsun's Z was now well established; Toyota's Celica was not quite the sophisticated machine their Supra has since become, but was on the way; the Porsche 911 was still the stuff of legend and their front-engined 924/928 series was about to create some more. Never had the need for a new Corvette been more vital.

To begin with the initial thinking was still based around the mid-engine concept that had been on the stocks (and off them, and then back on them . . .) for about 20 years. The starting point was the old four-rotor car, which metamorphosed into Bill Mitchell's Aerovette show car and which was widely believed by industry watchers to be at least the basis of the new-shape Corvette if not the actual thing: it had happened often enough in the past. Robbed of its Wankel rotary, the objective was to replace the powerplant with a conventional piston engine, either the existing smallblock V8 or one of the new-generation V6 engines just going through the factory, and work progressed in this direction. In fact it got so far down the line that the Aerovette was readied for production for the 1980 model year, but that was as close as it ever came.

In the end the problems associated with a volume-produced mid-engine design began to outnumber the advantages. Although there are a number of successful mid-engined cars they are still regarded as exotics by their makers, their drivers and their mechanics. The only volume-built sportscars that approach this configuration are truthfully rear-engined. In any case they tend to be small and nippy funsters rather than fast supercars, rather like Fiat's pretty and workable X-19. Only recently have Toyota launched the MR2 and Panther their Escort-based Solo.

In the late seventies, however, and particularly after Porsche announced that the successor to the 911 would be a conventional design featuring a front-mounted, water-cooled V8, the traditional layout seemed to be the best way in which Corvette could continue to offer the same standards to its buyers. Switching to a mid-engined

Below: New crisp styling for 1984 still shows traditional Corvette aura. The new dash *(top right)* includes all the digital technology learnt from the show cars and experimentals over the years.

CORVETTE

THE EIGHTIES AND BEYOND

layout would complicate the issue at what was probably the worst possible moment in its history. So instead it was decided to improve the package. The object then was to make Corvette smaller externally, bigger internally, get it under the gas-guzzler tax threshold, load it with as much technical, electronic and engineering sophistication as it could carry, and also give it improved performance and handling.

In that simplified design brief the decision to move upmarket was clearly and immediately apparent. Corvette policy had always been to raise its price when it was selling well, and during the late seventies that was an extreme understatement. From 41,673 in 1976, Corvette sales had shown a noticeable upward trend: 49,213 in 1977, down a little in 1978 to 46,776, and finally up to a record new figure of 53,807 in 1979. Base price of the new car when it was announced was well up on the 1982 models; by the time it moved into showrooms it was carrying a hefty $5,000 increase over the model it replaced. What is more, Chevrolet surveys showed that the strategy was right on target. Still selling all they could make, the median income of a Corvette buyer was up to around $70,000 a year, the average age now up to 40, and almost half the buyers were executives, salesmen, lawyers, even a few judges, putting Corvette right in there among the exoticar owners. And as further proof that it was right on the button, the level of trade-ins of expensive foreign exotics was three times up over the '82 models. Corvette was scoring heavy points in the target area; from being America's first sportscar in the fifties it had gone on against strong opposition to be America's premier sportscar in the sixties and seventies. Now it was America's first and only supercar.

CORVETTE

Now it was competing against Porsche and Ferrari in a way that it never had before, on level terms in every area except one: it was still far cheaper, at approximately half their price. It was launched in 1983, but built to a 1984 specification, so there was officially no 1983 Corvette, although the '82 was still available, staying in production right up to the end of 1982. Chevrolet had to choose between the chance to produce a 30th anniversary model or get the 1984 car into the market as soon as possible. The cars of the eighties had already been given about as much dress-up as they could reasonably stand, and the market for specials and 'Limited Editions' had been tapped almost to exhaustion. So they chose instead to have the car out nice and early for the model year, although it had been expected, even eagerly awaited, almost since the beginning of the decade.

Bowling Green closed down in October 1982 and work on retooling the factory began at the same time as the first pre-production cars became available. The 1984 Corvette was shown publicly early in the spring of 1983, went on sale in California in April on the same day as Chevrolet released the embargo to the press, and went on sale in the

Left: 1984 models still have that certain Corvette quality of line which has existed for 25 years.
Above: Twin rear lights preserve Corvette identity.
Below: The new clamshell bonnet gives better engine access.

THE EIGHTIES AND BEYOND

The steeply raked windshield helps Corvette to its lowest-ever 0.34 Cd.

CORVETTE

All pictures: The massive applications of engineering technology take the '84 Corvette into the 140mph supercar bracket, and lightweight aluminum is added to fiberglass.

CORVETTE

rest of the United States in March, although it was October before the plant was up to full-speed production.

Initial reaction to the new car was favorable and everybody at GM must have breathed a collective sigh of relief. The old shape had been around so long that it was hard to conceive of a Corvette looking any different, and the initial reaction to the new car was a big hurdle to be overcome.

What Palmer and the rest of Chevrolet Design Studio 111 had achieved was to bring Corvette's looks right up to date for the eighties without losing any of the essential character of the car. From a Palmer sketch the first full-size clay was finished in late 1978 and the final clay, barring details, was ready a year later. From the front, side or rear the new car was different in every way to the old, yet anyone seeing it for the first time would know instantly what he was looking at. Palmer said that he believed he and McLellan (who had worked closely together every step of the way) had designed a car 'without compromises, but we've managed to retain Corvette identity'.

One of the main design factors was aerodynamics. Although the old shape Corvette was one of the swoopiest-looking designs on the road, its aerodynamics weren't really that good. The new shape went through one of the most rigorous aerodynamic testing programs it's possible to organize, and included careful measurement of the pressure variations in the car's wake. Aerodynamicists are nowadays aware that the behavior of the airflow as it leaves the rear of a vehicle – 'separation' – is almost as critical to a good drag coefficient as its behavior at the front, and certainly is the most important influence on the car's straightline stability at speed. Shaping of the rear spoiler, the cutaway back and the curve of the rear valance panel provides, if you

THE EIGHTIES AND BEYOND

like, a tail for the arrow. And since an improvement to handling was a critical part of the design brief, this was an area that received great attention. This is a technique which GM, using computer-aided design, has since perfected to an even higher degree, but the Corvette was the first car ever to be designed using this method.

In the end the '84 came home with an overall drag factor of 0.34, 23 percent better than the 0.44 of the 1982 car but not as low as it could be. It is within the bounds of possibility that it could be reduced still further, making an 0.30 Cd a production reality some time in the future. But 0.34 is a respectable number and is a figure that influences handling, performance and gas mileage. The reduction was achieved by making it smaller than the old car in every dimension except width, and reducing its frontal area. The most visible evidence of this is in the steep 64-degree rake of the windshield, a 'faster' line than before and in fact the sharpest ever in the American auto industry.

The extra two inches of width give it more interior room than before, plus a wider track which gives more handling stability and allows it to develop phenomenal lateral g-forces in skidpan testing. At 176in overall, its length is down by almost 9in on its 96in wheelbase, which is two less than previously. Although it has a roofline an inch lower than the 1982 car the interior headroom is marginally better, at just over 36in. Legroom, too, is slightly up, but the extra width gives it a massive 6in improvement at shoulder height.

Much of the improvement to interior space is the result of the new chassis. Corvette has ridden a ladder-type chassis with crossmembers between its side rails supporting engine, transmission and axles, since its inception in 1952. The occasional spaceframe chassis that have appeared on Corvette specials are too complicated to make them viable for volume production, but the backbone chassis which was the heart of the mid-engined XP cars is ideal, and it is a variant of this that now carries Corvette.

On top of it goes a robot-welded birdcage assembly which gives torsional strength and provides a frame for the body panels to be mounted to. This 'uniframe', as GM call it, is another big departure for Corvette, which has been of body-on-frame construction since 1953. And that is not its only innovation, for the frame itself makes wide use of aluminum members to save weight. Although the finished car came out about 300lbs heavier than the engineers expected it was still 170lbs less than the 1982 model.

In fact Chevrolet claim that more aluminum is used in the new Corvette than in any other automobile in the past. The rigidity of its backbone frame is provided by an aluminum C-section beam which joins the engine/transmission assembly rigidly to the differential, and the propshaft housed within the 'C' is also of aluminum. Some suspension components are also made in aluminum – upper and lower control arms at front and rear, and the lateral control arm at the rear.

Extensive use of aluminum is also made in large numbers of smaller ancillaries. Some brake parts, the brake master cylinder, the air-conditioning compressor, the power steering and alternator brackets, and even the engine lifting bracket, are all aluminum. The transmission casing is made from aluminum sheet and the radiator from a mix of aluminum and plastic.

There was also extensive use of plastic elsewhere to save weight. The transverse rear spring, which had been part of Duntov's IRS design for the 1963 Corvette, had been changed during the 1981 production run; it was still a transverse leaf, but was now a single piece of fiberglass. Not only did it weigh half of the original item, but it was also tested as having a lifespan at least 66 times greater than steel. So successful was it at the rear that it was introduced at the front as well on the 1984 Corvette, in conjunction with the well-tried SLA (Short – Long Arm) arrangement.

According to Dave McLellan there was never any moment when a material other than glassfiber was seriously considered for the new Corvette bodyshell. Although it is an expensive technique, the rust-free body thus produced is exceptionally strong and virtually as light as aluminum sheet. By the same token there was no chance at all that Corvette would revert to a convertible option, since the weight penalties are simply too great to be considered.

The choice of powerplant for the new Corvette was made early on, and a revised version of the faithful 350 smallblock V8 is what still lives under its clamshell hood. There has been much experimentation with the smaller V6 engines, and some sages were predicting that the new Corvette would almost certainly be thus kitted out. But preservation of the V8 'heart' was seen as an essential part of continuing the Corvette traditions and identity into the eighties. In any case there was little chance that any V6 powerplant could provide Corvette with the kind of performance that would allow it to keep up with the supercars against which it was ranged.

This attitude was more than borne out by the figures when Corvette was tested by the press: the 1984 cars were easily good for 140mph, and needed to be against the competition. They were still the fastest thing built on the United States mainland and were faster than a great

Right: 1984 Corvette (*above right*) lines up with its illustrious predecessors for a display of sporting heritage any auto maker in the world would be proud of. The ladder chassis is replaced by a backbone of C-section aluminum (*below*).

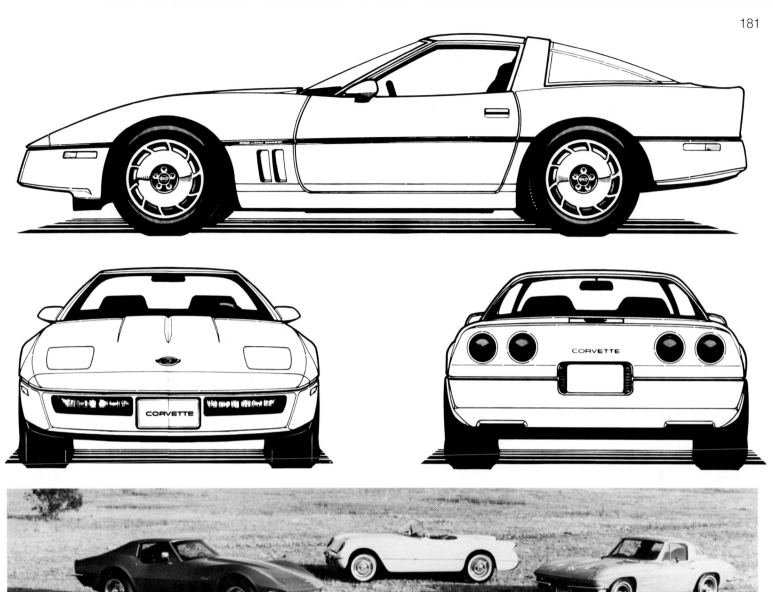

THE EIGHTIES AND BEYOND

deal of foreign exotics which cost two and three times as much. Chevrolet general manager Robert Stempel said it was a 'world class sportscar'; Dave McLellan said, 'this car will be at home and respected on the (limit-free) autobahn or any highway in the world'.

The V8 was some 5hp up on the '82 unit's output, largely thanks to the adoption of an electric fan and a new serpentine-drive belt system which drew less parasitic power from the engine. There was also the 'Crossfire' throttle-body fuel-injection system, which was not a complete and unmitigated success; 1985 models reverted to a port injection system which worked rather better. It meant saying farewell to the flat cast magnesium air cleaner which had dominated the engine compartment of the '84 and had been designed by Palmer & co to match the rest of the car. In fact under-hood cosmetics had played an important part in design, to the point at which AC Delco had been consulted on colors for the plug leads and had been persuaded to supply a version of their 'Freedom' battery in a special, matching color scheme.

Now, for the first time since 1981, Corvette standard transmission was a manual four-speed; the four-speed overdrive automatic from the previous year was carried over as an option. Even the manual transmission now included a large number of the new electronic packages which had become a part of the new Corvette. In this case it was a computer-controlled overdrive arrangement, which was a secondary gearset attached to the usual box. Operating on each gear except first through a hydraulic clutch it had the effect of improving

All pictures: The 1985 Corvette improves ride and roadholding yet further and lifts a stock Corvette above 150mph once again. Gentle suspension retuning has eliminated previous complaints about roadability and 'Crossfire' injection is replaced.

CORVETTE

fuel economy at part-throttle opening, and it could be switched out manually by a control on the center console. For all-out performance it was possible to order a higher rear axle ratio, 3.31:1, which gave it a better standing start take off.

It also came with the tougher Z51 suspension option, called the 'gymkhana' package; and it was with this that the amazing 0.95 lateral g could be racked up, although it had considerable ride penalties. From the beginning, the new Corvette had been engineered around its handling characteristics; the powerplant existed, styling was progressing and handling was what needed closest examination. The Pirelli P7 tires were chosen as the ones that demonstrated the qualities necessary to make Corvette handle in the way McLellan felt it should and, working closely with Goodyear, these capabilities were built into the Eagles with which the 1984 Corvette was equipped. With their great width and larger footprint these tires gave better results — even better resistance to aquaplaning — than previously.

Tire requirements were a low rolling resistance, high lateral strength, fast heat dissipation, good wet handling properties and low road noise, and Goodyear came up with the 130mph-rated design which incorporated much from their Formula One rain tire. These are an essential part of the handling package, to the extent that Chief Engineer McLellan said that 'the handling of the car is dominated by its tires as well as its structural integrity'.

The rear suspension was redesigned for the 1984 cars, and Duntov's setup was scrapped, replaced by an all-new 5-link arrangement incorporating all that aluminum and having better anti-squat and anti-dive qualities. A stabilizer bar at the front was standard, with a thicker bar, plus stiffer shock absorbers as part of the handling package.

Inside, the Corvette had a brand-new interior which features as its centerpiece an all-electronic digital display backed up by an electronic analog display, with bar charts monitoring engine revs and assorted other functions. This was another aspect of the growing influence of the microchip in the automobile, and was just part of the on-board computer management system.

With its T-top replaced by a one-piece clip-off (which could at last be stored inside the moving car without being damaged), with its 'handed' wheels with slotted air vents which only work if the wheel is on the correct side of the car, and its optional power seats, this was the 1984 Corvette unveiled before the world in the spring of 1983.

Production at the St Louis plant ended on July 31, 1981, when Corvette number 695,124 rolled off the line. It then switched to the bigger, modern, computerized facility at Bowling Green, Kentucky, in preparation for the new model. When production of the l982 cars ended the total figure stood at 729,844 Corvettes built since production had started at Flint 29 years earlier, and with a massive investment in plant and tooling Chevrolet (and the whole of GM) awaited the verdict following the unveiling of the first all-new Corvette for 20 years.

The first impressions were overwhelmingly good, and the magazine testers rushed home from the GM launch days in order to pass on the good news as fast as possible.

They then began to receive their long-term test cars and get to grips with them on a more intimate basis, and it was here again that everything started to go somewhat awry. As in the past the first cars off the line in production were not up to the standard that the examples first shown to the press had been. In a lot of cases the press at large felt that looks and performance aside, the '84 cars weren't up to the standard of the '82 models. Once again the outgoing cars had been given years to settle into a happy production-line routine, and despite all the planning and preparations the new cars were having their own teething troubles.

As had happened before, the principal complaint seemed to center on quality control and in particular on the same old bugbears: the new Corvette was noisy and harsh out in the real world. Beyond any doubts at all it still delivered performance and could be proved of its

handling in any company in the world, but there was a price to pay. While describing it as 'an F-15 for the road' *Car and Driver* slammed its ride, especially the Z51 setup which, they said, 'ruins the car for day-to-day use'. Some magazine writers found that even the base suspension package was too harsh for them, and would have preferred a quieter ride with less road and exhaust noise as well as less bouncing.

One thing that seemed to have atracted criticism right from the beginning was the instrumentation, and closer acquaintance seemed to turn reservation into dislike, mostly on the grounds of illegibility, especially in bright sunlight. Part of the rejection of the system seemed to center around a rather prejudiced belief that it was un-

CORVETTE

Above: Totally revamped 1984 Corvette with clamshell roof.
Top left: Extensive use of aluminium throughout helps keep weight down.
Left: The low front aspect is wider than the old shape but still offers less drag.

necessarily 'flashy' and had been selected simply to point out the high-tech nature of the vehicle.

But, like everybody else, *Car and Driver* ended their story with a round of applause for the Corvette's performance, with 60mph coming up from rest in about 7 seconds, 140mph arriving at full stretch and a dazzling handling capability in between which made it at least the equal of any other series production automobile in the world.

Given previous Corvette history, it was logical that the 1985 Corvette should be even better than the 1984 had been. The work had been going on for some while and principally involved continual minor tweaking. Walt Banacki was the king of the NVH patrols who de-rattled the down-sized GM cars of the late seventies. He made 200 suggestions for minor changes to Corvette which would quieten it down, and GM said that 90 percent of them were adopted. While the interior was being reworked the dash graphics were redesigned for improved legibility. Both the base suspension and the Z51 option were softened up to make Corvette a little more relaxed and civilized.

Minor engine changes to the breathing and the change from throttle-body injection system to a port injection setup, plus clever techniques with the computerized engine management arrangements also gave Corvette more power for 1985. The numbers went up from 205hp in 1984 to 230hp in 1985. Along with the suspension

changes an alteration in ride height dropped the drag figure down to 0.33. Also on the scene for the '85 cars was a 3.07:1 back axle. What all this meant in practice was that Corvette now went a little faster while remaining on the safe side of the EPA threshold.

In fact the slogan among Corvette people in late 1984 was 'life begins at 150'. For the first time in over a decade it was possible to buy a showroom stock Corvette that could put a genuine 150mph mark on its speedometer – and sustain it. The automatic transmission cars jump from 0-60mph in under 6 seconds, and run the standing quarter in 14 seconds, 97mph.

Even with all the improvements there were still reservations among the press testers, mostly centered around the belief that the suspension, although it functioned as well as any other auto maker's, was still a little on the stiff side. The reason was that although GM were still officially not involved in motor racing there were those at Corvette who felt that the new car was, in showroom trim, ready to race and capable of upholding an honorable tradition in the SCCA Showroom Stock class. Suspension trimming and tuning for the 1985 car was carried out at Firebird Raceway in Arizona. The 1985 engine cut a second off the lap times, and suspension work reduced them by another second – which is why the ride was still a bit lumpy.

But, upholding another honorable tradition, test drives in the 1985 Corvette caused *Car and Driver* to say that the reworked 1985 model was 'the Corvette we wished for in the first place'.

When he'd finished the design work on the 1984 Corvette Jerry Palmer said that it would be around for some time. Not as long as the

CORVETTE

Top left: The ZR1 'King of the Hill' (front).
Below left: Something for everyone in this line up.
Top: Aluminum wheels are slotted to duct air, and are 'handed' to fit one side of the car only.
Above: Crossfire injection looked good, worked less well and has now been dropped.

with computer-controlled active ride suspension – something which continued to thwart GM engineers, as well as many of the people attempting to get it right for racetrack applications in Grand Prix. And there was an air of racebred excitement in the mid-eighties. GM found that on-board electronics could help reach performance figures not dreamed of since the oil crisis.

The electronic engine management packages were microchip controlled, adjusting fuel injection and spark timing as much as 100 times a second. When the knock sensor was combined with a management computer, cars could run on unleaded gas at 10.5:1 compression ratios without damage, and suddenly horsepower figures were on the way up again. And that in engines which could be certified at 22.5mpg and pass all the current and anticipated smog regulations. The Crossfire fuel injection was replaced by a proper multipoint system, helping Corvette showroom stock performance back up to 150mph, with the promise of more in sight. But those weren't the only improvements. The press had, as always, slammed the build quality of the 1984 production cars as harsh, noisy, full of rattles and fragile. Almost 200 changes took the rattles and thumps out of the car, and the suspension was softened to meet driver criticism.

With the 150mph road car back in the showrooms for 1986, Corvette people turned back to the racetrack. The IMSA GTP Corvette was the first result, a prototype styled in the wind tunnel by Jerry Palmer's team and bearing almost no resemblance to the road cars outside, still less under the hood. It was powered by an Ilmor-developed turbo V6 which was at the heart of the GM return to racing – under the banner of Budweiser, Penske and anybody else but GM.

In 1987 the Ilmor Chevy engine was sent to do battle in Indy CART racing; among the fastest, it was also the least reliable, and turned 1987 into a year of humiliation. But a full effort over the winter changed the picture completely and in 1988 the Ilmor-Chevy cars took 14 out of 15 pole positions, 14 out of 15 wins. Danny Sullivan's Penske Chevy drive gave him the title, Al Unser Jr took his Ilmor-Chevy-powered car into second spot and Rick Mears brought the second Ilmor-Chevy Pennzoil car home fourth. Chevrolet was a performance name to reckon with, and Corvette backed it absolutely, first with a fabulously good-looking convertible, and then by what must remain as the tour de force of Corvette's forty-year story. The car that everyone was talking about was shown to Chevrolet dealers in Arizona in the spring of 1988, and orders were placed on the spot.

Group Lotus had helped develop a multi-valve, multi-cam version of the 350 V8 engine, and it was placed into the Corvette along with a six-speed ZF manual gearbox and a hatful of electronics. The engineers had just missed their targets of 400hp and 400lb/ft of torque: the new Corvette had 'about' 380hp and 370lb/ft. No official figures were quoted at its launch, but when the ZR-1 was shown to the press at Milford in the spring of 1989 it launched itself from 0-60mph in just 4.2 seconds. The gearbox ratios means that maximum speed of 'about' 180mph is reached in fifth: the sixth gear is an overdrive ratio which gives the ZR1 a theoretical speed of 306mph. Unsurprisingly this car had been dubbed 'King of the Hill' long before its launch, despite Dave McLellan's protests.

The ZR1 has a lockable electronic 'valet' setting which limits it to 'only' 200hp by operating only eight inlet ports. In full power mode, another eight ports are opened, and are fed by cam lobes with a longer duration than the initial eight, adding peak power to the mid-range torque of the 'valet' setting.

Almost as soon as the ZR-1 went public, GM Europe announced an upmarket version of their Omega/Carlton range. This sports saloon had a 3.6 24-valve straight six, two turbos, three coils, no distributor at all, and developed 360hp and 376lbs/ft maximum torque through twin catalytic converters – and there was a new multi-link independent rear suspension. It was called the Lotus Carlton, and was unmistakably the handiwork of the Hethel engineers. Quite clearly it showed that the low-capacity six-cylinder engine could be made to deliver the goods and stay within fuel consumption and emission control requirements. It pointed the way ahead for Corvette – and all of the General's performance cars. Surely the next Corvette would be a mid-engine V6. . .

last one, but certainly it would be the shape which took Corvette into the nineties. At the time it was launched, Dave McLellan said that he didn't anticipate major changes in Corvette until the nineties.

However all that changed in 1988 with the appearance of the futuristic mid-engined Corvette Indy. Reeking of every previous mid-engine show car, with more than a hint of banana-shaped Italian streamlining, the Indy was a project for the future, said Chevrolet, while failing to comment on its startling similarity to the Buick Wildcat – which was actually a running special rather than a static show car. But by then, plenty of other things had changed too. In 1984, Dave McLellan was talking about on-board electronics as being the most important innovation for at least 20 years. Not just for engine management systems, but in ABS, electronic ride control, power steering, in fact, virtually anything. By that time GM was the largest computer manufacturer in the world, most of its output destined for on-board applications in cars and trucks.

What Dave McLellan may have known was that GM had its eye on Group Lotus in Britain, largely because of the company's progress

Workers at the Corvette plant at Bowling Green, Kentucky, which opened June 1st, 1981.

Index

192

R
Rathman, Jim, driver 48
rear window divider 56, 72, 75, 83, 89
Road and Track magazine 93, 98, 100, 114
road/race development program 17, 21, 41, 43, 44, 45, 48-9, 64
roll up window introduced 36

S
Sales figures, Corvette
  1953 28
  1954 27-8, 29
  1955 44, 49
  1956 44
  1957 45, 48, 49
  1958 49
  1959 53
  1961, 1962 61
  1963 76, 93
  1964 93
  1965 97, 100
  1966, 1967 99-100
  1968 114, 141
  1969 123
  1970, 1972 141
  1973 123, 124
  1974, 1975 143
  1976, 1977 146, 174
  1978, 1979 174

sales, figures, Ford 33, 49
SCCA meetings 43, 45, 48, 53, 57, 65, 88, 100, 156, 157, 185
Sebring meetings 43, 45, 48, 67, 83, 93, 100, 152, 155
selling prices
  Ford Thuderbird 29
  Jaguar 21, 26
  MG 21, 26, 28
  Porsche 21, 26
selling prices, Corvette
  target price 13, 21
  1953 26
  1954 28
  1956 41, 44
  1957 45
  1959 53
  1963 76
  1970 128
  1973 135
  1975 143
  1978 147
  1983 174
Shelby, Carroll 44, 61, 65, 76, 80, 88, 155
  Cobra 65, 76, 83, 88
  427 Cobra 89, 99
Shinoda, Larry, stylist 71, 105, 156, 159, 163
side scallops 36-7, 57, 61, 75
Skelton, Betty, driver 42

Sloan, Alfred P 10, 11, 13, 57
Sports Car Graphic magazine 98
steering 18, 92
Stempel, Robert 182

T
Tailfins 13
Targa Florio 43, 82
Taruffi, Piero 155
Thiebaud, Ed, collector 125
Thompson, Dr Richard 42-3, 45, 57, 67, 88
  and Sting Ray 71, 156-7
Thompson, Mickey 76, 97
Toyota 172
transmission
  Borg Warner 4-speed 45, 57
  Muncie 4-speed manual 89, 99, 109, 135
  Powerglide 2-speed auto 20, 26, 28, 57, 76
  Saginaw 3-speed 99
Tritt, William 12

W
Wankel rotary engine 17, 29, 167, 169, 172
Watkins Glen race meetings 88
wraparound wind shield 13, 17, 36, 55

Picture Credits
Robert Baldridge: front jacket (inset right), pages 170-1.
GM/Chevrolet Motor Division: pages 4-5, 6-7, 8-9, 10, 11 (both), 12, 13, 14 (both), 15 (both), 16, 17 (both), 26-7, 27, 29, 32, 34-5, 36, 36-7, 37, 38 (top left & right), 40-1, 41, 42, 43, 44-5, 45, 48 (both), 49, 53, 57 (top), 64 (both), 65, 66 (bottom), 67 (top left & right), 68 (bottom left & right), 68-9, 70-1, 72, 73 (all three), 77, 80, 81, 82, 82-3, 84, 84-5, 88, 89, 90, 90-1, 91, 92, 92-3, 96, 96-7, 100-1, 101, 104 (both), 106-7, 112-13, 118, 118-19, 119 (both), 122, 122-3, 125, 126-7, 128 (top), 130 (both), 131, 134, 134-5, 136, 138-9, 142-3, 143, 146, 146-7, 148-9, 150-1, 152-3, 153, 154-5, 155, 156, 157 (both), 158 (both), 159 (both), 160-1, 162 (both), 163, 164 (both), 165, 166 (top), 166-7, 167, 167 (top left & right), 168, 168-9, 169, 172-3, 173, 174, 175 (both), 176-7, 178 (both), 178-9, 179 (both), 180, 181 (both), 182 (both), 183 (all three), 184 (both), 185, 186 (both), 187 (both), 188-9.
Haymarket Publications: front jacket (main photo).
UPI/Bettmann Newsphotos: page 105.
Nicky Wright: front jacket (inset left), back jacket, pages 1, 2-3, 7, 18-19 (all five), 20-1, 22-3, 24, 25 (both), 28, 30-1 (all four), 32-3, 33, 38-9, 39, 46-7, 50, 50-1, 51, 52, 54, 54-5, 56 (both), 57 (bottom), 58-9, 60-1, 61, 62-3, 66 (top), 67 (bottom), 70 (bottom), 71 (both), 74 (both), 74-5, 75 (both), 76-7, 78-9, 83, 86, 86-7, 87, 98 (top left & right), 98-9, 99, 102 (both), 102-3, 103, 107, 108 (both), 109 (all three), 110-1 (twelve), 114 (both), 115, 116, 116-17, 117 (both), 120-1, 123, 124, 124-5, 128 (bottom), 129 (both), 132 (bottom left & right), 132-3, 135, 136-7, 139, 140, 140-1, 141, 144-5, back flap.